*The Eternal Dice*

César Vallejo

# The Eternal Dice
## selected poems

*translated from the Spanish*
*by Margaret Jull Costa*

A NEW DIRECTIONS
PAPERBOOK ORIGINAL

Manufactured in the United States of America
First published as New Directions Paperbook 1626 in 2025

*Library of Congress Cataloging-in-Publication Data*
Names: Vallejo, César, 1892–1938, author. | Costa, Margaret Jull, translator. |
Vallejo, César, 1892–1938. Eternal dice. |
Vallejo, César, 1892–1938. Eternal dice. Spanish.
Title: The eternal dice : selected poems / by César Vallejo ;
translated by Margaret Jull Costa.
Other titles: Eternal dice (Compilation)
Description: First edition. | New York : New Directions Publishing, 2025.
Identifiers: LCCN 2024045627 | ISBN 9780811237666 (paperback) |
ISBN 9780811237673 (ebook)
Subjects: LCSH: Vallejo, César, 1892–1938—Translations into English. |
LCGFT: Poetry.
Classification: LCC PQ8497.V35 E8413 2025 | DDC 861/.62—dc23/eng/20241016
LC record available at https://lccn.loc.gov/2024045627

10 9 8 7 6 5 4 3 2 1

New Directions Books are published for James Laughlin
by New Directions Publishing Corporation
80 Eighth Avenue, New York 10011

# Table of Contents

# Translator's introduction

Many English-language translators have been drawn to César Vallejo's work, perhaps because translators are naturally, and possibly masochistically, drawn to the difficult, to writers who use language in complex, innovative ways, and whose work can seemingly defy translation. My version of this selection of Vallejo's work is yet another attempt to do the impossible, always bearing in mind Beckett's advice: fail again, fail better.

César Abraham Vallejo was born in 1892 in Santiago de Chuco, a small Andean town in northern Peru. He was the youngest of eleven children, and, as can be seen from several of the poems included in this selection, his was a very close family. He went to school in Santiago, and although he later enrolled in university in the regional capital, Trujillo, he failed to complete his first year, finding work instead in a copper mine, mining being the main industry in the area. The following year, he again enrolled in a university, this time in the capital Lima, but was once more unable to continue because of financial difficulties. He subsequently worked as a tutor to a wealthy mining family, as an assistant cashier on a sugar plantation—an experience that opened his eyes to the plight of exploited workers—and then as a teacher, a job that finally allowed him to complete his university studies. In 1914, he began to publish his poems in local newspapers and magazines, and became involved in various literary circles, discovering (in translation) the work of the French symbolists, as well as Walt Whitman, and, more especially, the Nicaraguan poet Rubén Darío. After graduating in 1915, he obtained a teaching post at a prestigious school in Lima. There he had a tempestuous affair with the sister-in-law of a colleague (Vallejo's biographer Juan Espejo Asturrizaga declined to give her full name, but her identity was later revealed to be Otilia Villanueva Gonzales). However, when Vallejo refused to marry her, she went to live in another town. This scandalous affair ultimately lost him his job, leaving him, once again, with no means of support. Nevertheless, in 1919, he published his first book of poems, *Los heraldos negros*, which, however, received only a lukewarm reception.*

In 1920, on a visit to his home town to attend a local celebration, a fight broke out, during which the premises of one of the town's most prominent businesses was set on fire and ransacked. A bystander was shot and two policemen were killed. Vallejo was accused of being one of the rioters, and after going into hiding at a friend's house, he was arrested and put in prison for 112 days before being released, case unproven. While in jail, he wrote several of the poems that later formed part of his collection *Trilce*, which was published in 1922, once more to a very cool reception.

In 1923, when it seemed likely that the lawsuit against him might be reopened, Vallejo decided to leave for Paris, as many of his fellow Latin American artists and writers did at the time. His first two years there were very hard, a constant struggle to earn enough money to live on. Indeed, he fell seriously ill and was hospitalized for over a month. He was saved by three things: a monthly commission from the Bureau des Grands Journaux Ibéro-Américains, the money he earned for articles about Parisian life written for two Lima-based magazines, *Mundial* and *Variedades*, and a study grant from the Spanish

* The book was finished a year before, but was delayed while Vallejo waited, in vain, for his friend Abraham Valdelomar to write an introduction.

government. Vallejo never had any intention of studying in Madrid, but he did go there three times to pick up the grant money. Meanwhile, he became part of Parisian cultural life and, with his friend Juan Larrea, founded a very short-lived avant-garde magazine. He also began a relationship with a young dressmaker, Henriette Maisse, with whom he lived for two years, before embarking on a parallel affair with a neighbor's daughter, Georgette de Phillipart, finally choosing to move in with Georgette when her mother died, leaving her a small legacy. He sent Georgette to break the news to Henriette.

Like many of the French surrealists of the time, he was drawn to Marxism, and read widely on the subject. When, in 1928, the Peruvian government granted him a free passage back to Peru, he took the money and spent it instead on a tour of Europe, taking in Berlin, Moscow, and Budapest. In 1929, Vallejo returned to Moscow, this time with Georgette, visiting Leningrad, Prague, and Vienna along the way. He wrote regular columns for a Spanish review about his experiences in Russia, and later turned these into a book, *Rusia en 1931*, which actually sold quite well. Vallejo cut short a third visit to Russia, apparently having become disillusioned with the Stalinist policies of the time, and having fallen out with the Moscow-based International Union of Revolutionary Writers.

A Spanish friend suggested that Vallejo allow a Madrid publisher to bring out a second edition of *Trilce*, and, after he was expelled from France for his political activities, he and Georgette moved to Madrid. He returned to France illegally to rejoin Georgette when she traveled back to Paris, and was told he could only stay if he ceased all political activity and reported to the prefecture every month. After a few months, this restriction was lifted and he was granted leave to stay. At which point, he and Georgette married.

With the outbreak of the Civil War in Spain in 1936, Vallejo became passionately involved in the Republican cause, writing articles in support of the Republic and making two visits to Madrid, first as a reporter, and later as the Peruvian delegate at the Second International Writers Congress in 1937. These visits only confirmed his fears that the Republican side would lose the war, but he appears also to have experienced a burst of creativity, writing, in the space of just eighty-six days, twenty-three of the poems in *Poemas humanos* and the fifteen poems of *España, aparta de mí este cáliz* (both collections were published posthumously).

Then, in 1938, Vallejo fell ill again, and the doctors were unable to find the cause. He died a month later. The cause of his death was given as an intestinal infection, but there has been much speculation as to the "real" cause. Was it grief for what seemed to be the inevitable defeat of the Republic in Spain? Or malaria or syphilis or simply exhaustion? And since he died on Good Friday, some even saw him as a kind of Christ figure. Stephen M. Hart has recently suggested that Vallejo was poisoned by the Russians after he became disillusioned with Soviet politics and was labeled by them as a Trotskyist. We will probably never know the truth.

His widow, Georgette, devoted the rest of her life to finding publishers for his poems and essays, and was responsible for putting together the two collections: *Poemas humanos* and *España, aparta de mí este cáliz*. She eventually went to live permanently in Peru, where she died in 1984.

Out of this brief but difficult life came these often very difficult poems. I first read a selection of them when I was at university, using James Higgins's excellent anthology. I still have my own annotated copy, full of my eager attempts to understand these often gnomic poems. Then, a few years ago, I led a couple of translation workshops at Nottingham University, admittedly working on two of the rather simpler poems, and this filled me with a desire to translate more of them. Vallejo's more transparent poems, often addressed to his parents and his family, were less problematic, but as I burrowed deeper in, from the *Trilce* poems on, but before that too, I came to appreciate that what he is confronting—namely, human misery, isolation, anguish, and his own sense of helplessness in the face of all that—is basically beyond words, beyond imagery. We translators spend our lives trying to understand, to interpret, but here, I realized, I simply had to translate what was there, however obscure or nonsensical, such strange pairings as "bromidic slopes," "nubile campaign," "pancreatic fingers," or entirely new words, with Vallejo turning nouns into verbs—*dos aguas encontradas que jamás han de istmarse* becomes "two opposing waters that will remain for ever unisthmused"—or combining two adjectives into one, *tembloroso* and *tenebroso* to make *tenebloso*, which, in English, becomes *tremebrous*. Or: *mi padre es una víspera*, literally, "my father is an eve," which has become in my slightly domesticated version: "my father is the eve of something." The poems are also full of grammatically illogical phrases: *El traje que vestí mañana*—"the suit I wore tomorrow"; or *me he sentado a caminar*—"I have just sat down to go walking." However, given Vallejo's world view, according to which injustice reigns supreme, and God, if he exists, is cruel, indifferent, and incapable of doing anything about that scourge Death (another constant presence in Vallejo's work), illogic seems the only logical response. Nor are his poems the fruit of some kind of automatic writing, for Vallejo edited and redrafted and honed his poetry. This is the only way in which he could describe the antithetical, paradoxical, oxymoronic universe he was living in, by using language at full tilt, making it perform all kinds of acrobatics. The resulting poems often defy interpretation, although this has not prevented a whole army of scholars from offering their interpretations, and to them, I must say, I am very grateful.

As I said at the start, very difficult poetry is often a magnet to translators (think of the numerous versions of Rilke's *Duino Elegies* or Baudelaire's *Fleurs du mal*), and I am yet another one. I feel indebted to those whose translations I occasionally consulted (James Higgins, Clayton Eshleman, Ed Dorn, and Gordon Brotherston), even if only to find consolation in discovering, given that understanding (in its usual translatorial sense) is often impossible, that they hadn't necessarily "understood" what Vallejo meant either. I was grateful for their companionship, though, because I could see that, like me, they had done their best to find an English echo, to communicate at least some of what is there in Vallejo's Spanish. What I hope comes across in my versions is, above all else, Vallejo's sheer verbal and intellectual energy, his intense engagement with language and life, his intense emotions, be it (out)rage or love or yearning, because much of the "meaning "of these poems lies precisely in that linguistic energy.

MARGARET JULL COSTA

# Acknowledgments

My heartfelt thanks to ...

Rebecca Hubbard, who patiently read my versions against the Spanish originals, and, applying her critical poetic eye, urged me to strip out any unnecessary words and resist domesticating the undomesticatable.

Professor Bernard McGuirk, who so generously read my versions more than once, comparing them with the originals and reading them as poems in their own right. His comments and suggestions were invaluable.

Professor Stephen M. Hart, who allowed me to use his excellent chronology (included in Clayton Eshleman's *Complete Poetry of César Vallejo*) as the basis for my own brief biography of Vallejo and made several useful comments on my introduction as a whole.

*The Eternal Dice*

## Los heraldos negros

Hay golpes en la vida, tan fuertes … Yo no sé!
Golpes como del odio de Dios; como si ante ellos,
la resaca de todo lo sufrido
se empozara en el alma … Yo no sé!

Son pocos; pero son … Abren zanjas oscuras
en el rostro más fiero y en el lomo más fuerte.
Serán tal vez los potros de bárbaros atilas;
o los heraldos negros que nos manda la Muerte.

Son las caídas hondas de los Cristos del alma,
de alguna fe adorable que el Destino blasfema.
Esos golpes sangrientos son las crepitaciones
de algún pan que en la puerta del horno se nos quema.

Y el hombre … Pobre … pobre! Vuelve los ojos, como
cuando por sobre el hombro nos llama una palmada;
vuelve los ojos locos, y todo lo vivido
se empoza, como charco de culpa, en la mirada.

Hay golpes en la vida, tan fuertes … Yo no sé!

## The Black Heralds

There are blows in life so hard ... I don't know!
Blows that feel like God's loathing; as if, beneath those blows,
the undertow of everything we've suffered
formed pools of pain in the soul ... I don't know!

They are few; but they're there ... They dig dark furrows
in the proudest of faces and the strongest of backs.
They are perhaps the horses of some barbarian attilas;
or the black heralds sent to us by Death.

They are the deep plunges into despair of the soul's Christs,
of some adorable faith blasphemed against by Fate.
Those bloody blows are the cracklings
of a loaf that burns as we take it from the oven.

And man ... Poor ... poor man! He glances round, as we might
when a summoning hand claps us on the shoulder,
he spins round, wild-eyed, and all he's ever lived
pools into puddles of guilt in that look.

There are blows in life so hard ... I don't know!

*Heces*

Esta tarde llueve, como nunca; y no
tengo ganas de vivir, corazón.

Esta tarde es dulce. Por qué no ha de ser?
Viste gracia y pena; viste de mujer.

Esta tarde en Lima llueve. Y yo recuerdo
las cavernas crueles de mi ingratitud;
mi bloque de hielo sobre su amapola,
más fuerte que su "No seas así!"

Mis violentas flores negras; y la bárbara
y enorme pedrada; y el trecho glacial.
Y pondrá el silencio de su dignidad
con óleos quemantes el punto final.

Por eso esta tarde, como nunca, voy
con este búho, con este corazón.

Y otras pasan; y viéndome tan triste,
toman un poquito de ti
en la abrupta arruga de mi hondo dolor.

Esta tarde llueve, llueve mucho. ¡Y no
tengo ganas de vivir, corazón!

## Dregs

This afternoon it's raining as never before; and,
my heart, I don't want to live.

This afternoon is sweet. And why wouldn't it be?
Dressed in grace and sorrow, dressed like woman.

This afternoon in Lima it's raining. And I remember
the cruel caverns of my ingratitude;
my block of ice on her poppy,
far stronger than her "Don't be like that!"

My violent black flowers; and the huge, cruel
stone blow; then the glacial pause.
Until, with burning oils, the silence of her dignity
will, at last, put the final full stop.

That is why, this afternoon, as never before, I
carry with me this reclusive owl, this heart.

Other women pass; and seeing me so sad,
they take a tiny bit of you lodged
in the sharp crease of my deep grief.

This afternoon it's raining, raining hard. And,
my heart, I don't want to live.

## Ágape

Hoy no ha venido nadie a preguntar;
ni me han pedido en esta tarde nada.

No he visto ni una flor de cementerio
en tan alegre procesión de luces.
Perdóname, Señor: qué poco he muerto!

En esta tarde todos, todos pasan
sin preguntarme ni pedirme nada.

Y no sé qué se olvidan y se queda
mal en mis manos, como cosa ajena.

He salido a la puerta,
y me da ganas de gritar a todos:
Si echan de menos algo, aquí se queda!

Porque en todas las tardes de esta vida,
yo no sé con qué puertas dan a un rostro,
y algo ajeno se toma el alma mía.

Hoy no ha venido nadie;
y hoy he muerto qué poco en esta tarde!

## Ágape

Today no one came to inquire; nor,
this evening, did anyone ask me for anything.

I didn't see a single graveyard flower
in such a joyful procession of lights.
Forgive me, Lord: how little I have died!

This evening everyone, everyone, walks past
without inquiring or asking me anything.

And yet something or other was left behind, it sits
awkwardly in my hands, as if it belonged to someone else.

I've gone over to the door,
and I feel like calling out to everyone:
If you've lost anything, it's here!

Because in all the evenings of this life,
I don't know which doors will be slammed in whose face,
and a something not mine grips my soul.

Today, no one came;
and today, this evening, how little I have died!

———

Borrowed partly from Latin and partly from Ancient Greek, *ágape*
was used in the early Christian church to mean love or charity, as
well as a communal meal.

*La de a mil*

El suertero que grita "La de a mil",
contiene no sé qué fondo de Dios.

Pasan todos los labios. El hastío
despunta en una arruga su yanó.
Pasa el suertero que atesora, acaso
nominal, como Dios,
entre panes tantálicos, humana
impotencia de amor.

Yo le miro al andrajo. Y él pudiera
darnos el corazón;
pero la suerte aquella que en sus manos
aporta, pregonando en alta voz,
como un pájaro cruel, irá a parar
adonde no lo sabe ni lo quiere
este bohemio dios.

Y digo en este viernes tibio que anda
a cuestas bajo el sol:
por qué se habrá vestido de suertero
la voluntad de Dios!

## The Winning Ticket

The lottery seller calling out, "Buy the winning ticket,"
has something of God about him.

All lips pass him by. Tedium
sprouts from a wrinkle in their "nothanks."
The lottery seller passes by, and he, perhaps nominally,
like God, keeps hoarded away,
among tantalizing loaves, the human
impotence for love.

I look at him, poor wretch. And to think
he could give us his heart;
but the lucky ticket in that bohemian god's hands,
as he loudly cries his wares,
like some cruel bird, will end up
where he neither knows nor cares.

And on this tepid Friday that walks along
carrying the sun on its back, I say:
why would the will of God dress up
as a lottery seller!

## El pan nuestro

Para Alejandro Gamboa

Se bebe el desayuno ... Húmeda tierra
de cementerio huele a sangre amada.
Ciudad de invierno ... La mordaz cruzada
de una carreta que arrastrar parece
una emoción de ayuno encadenada!

Se quisiera tocar todas las puertas,
y preguntar por no sé quién; y luego
ver a los pobres, y, llorando quedos,
dar pedacitos de pan fresco a todos.
Y saquear a los ricos sus viñedos
con las dos manos santas
que a un golpe de luz
volaron desclavadas de la Cruz!

Pestaña matinal, no os levantéis!
¡El pan nuestro de cada día dánoslo,
Señor ...!

Todos mis huesos son ajenos;
yo talvez los robé!
Yo vine a darme lo que acaso estuvo
asignado para otro;
y pienso que, si no hubiera nacido,
otro pobre tomara este café!
Yo soy un mal ladrón ... A dónde iré!

## Our Daily Bread

For Alejandro Gamboa

I drink my morning coffee ... The damp graveyard
soil smells of much-loved blood.
Winter city ... The acerbic creak of a passing
cart seems to bring with it
an unending sense of fasting!

It makes me feel like knocking on every door
and asking for someone, quite who, I don't know; and then
visiting the poor, and, weeping softly,
handing out little pieces of fresh bread to them all.
And plundering the vineyards of the rich
with two saintly hands
that, in a flash of light,
fly, unnailed, from the Cross!

Morning eyelids, don't open!
Give us this day our daily bread,
Lord ...!

All my bones belong to someone else;
perhaps I stole them!
I ended up giving myself what was perhaps
intended for another;
and I think, if I hadn't been born,
another poor soul would be drinking this coffee!
I'm a bad thief ... Where shall I go!

Y en esta hora fría, en que la tierra
trasciende a polvo humano y es tan triste,
quisiera yo tocar todas las puertas,
y suplicar a no sé quién, perdón,
y hacerle pedacitos de pan fresco
aquí, en el horno de mi corazón …!

And at this chill hour, in which the earth
gives off a smell of human dust and is so sad,
I wish I could knock on every door,
and beg someone's forgiveness, quite who, I don't know,
and bake little pieces of fresh bread for them
right here, in the oven of my heart ...!

## Absoluta

Color de ropa antigua. Un Julio a sombra,
y un Agosto recién segado. Y una
mano de agua que injertó en el pino
resinoso de un tedio malas frutas.

Ahora que has anclado, oscura ropa,
tornas rociada de un suntuoso olor
a tiempo, a abreviación ... Y he cantado
el proclive festín que se volcó.

Mas, ¿no puedes, Señor, contra la muerte,
contra el límite, contra lo que acaba?
Ay! la llaga en color de ropa antigua,
cómo se entreabre y huele a miel quemada!

Oh unidad excelsa! Oh lo que es uno
por todos!
Amor contra el espacio y contra el tiempo!
Un latido único de corazón;
un solo ritmo: Dios!

Y al encogerse de hombros los linderos
en un bronco desdén irreductible,
hay un riego de sierpes
en la doncella plenitud del 1.
¡Una arruga, una sombra!

## Final Discharge

The color of old clothes. A July in the shadows,
and an August cut short.* And a
heavy downpour that grafted rotten fruit
onto the resinous pine tree of tedium.

Now that you've dropped anchor, dark clothes,
you are again full of the sumptuous smell
of time, of abbreviation ... And I have sung
of the tilting banquet table that finally tipped over.

But, Lord, can't you do something about death,
about boundaries, about things ending?
Ay, that wound the color of old clothes,
how it gapes open and smells of burnt honey!

Ah, sublime unity! Ah, all the things that are the same
for everyone!
Love versus space and versus time!
A single beat of the heart;
one rhythm only: God!

And when the borders shrug their shoulders
in coarse irreducible disdain,
there is a flurry of serpents
in the virginal plenitude of 1.
A wrinkle, a shadow!

———

* In Peru, July and August are the winter months.

## Líneas

Cada cinta de fuego
que, en busca del Amor,
arrojo y vibra en rosas lamentables,
me da a luz el sepelio de una víspera.
Yo no sé si el redoble en que lo busco,
será jadear de roca,
o perenne nacer de corazón.

Hay tendida hacia el fondo de los seres,
un eje ultranervioso, honda plomada.
¡La hebra del destino!
Amor desviará tal ley de vida,
hacia la voz del Hombre;
y nos dará la libertad suprema
en transubstanciación azul, virtuosa,
contra lo ciego y lo fatal.

¡Que en cada cifra lata,
recluso en albas frágiles,
el Jesús aún mejor de otra gran Yema!

Y después ... La otra línea ...
Un Bautista que aguaita, aguaita, aguaita ...
Y, cabalgando en intangible curva,
un pie bañado en púrpura.

*Lines*


Every ribbon of fire
I hurl forth in search of Love
quivers among crumpled roses,
births me into the burial of a yet to be.
I don't know if the drumbeat in which I look for it
will be the gasping of a rock,
or the perennial coming into being of a heart.

Lying at the bottom of all beings,
an ultranervous axis, a deep plumb line.
Fate's thread!
Love will divert that law of life
towards the voice of Man;
and will give us supreme freedom,
through a virtuous, blue transubstantiation,
from blindness and the inevitable.

In every number
may an even better Jesus from another great Embryo
pulsate, imprisoned in fragile dawns!

And afterwards ... The other line ...
A John the Baptist who waits, waits, waits ...
And, riding past along an intangible curve,
a foot bathed in purple.

## La cena miserable

Hasta cuándo estaremos esperando lo que
no se nos debe … Y en qué recodo estiraremos
nuestra pobre rodilla para siempre! Hasta cuándo
la cruz que nos alienta no detendrá sus remos.

Hasta cuándo la Duda nos brindará blasones
por haber padecido!…
             Ya nos hemos sentado
mucho a la mesa, con la amargura de un niño
que a media noche, llora de hambre, desvelado …

Y cuándo nos veremos con los demás, al borde
de una mañana eterna, desayunados todos.
Hasta cuándo este valle de lágrimas, a donde
yo nunca dije que me trajeran.
                  De codos
todo bañado en llanto, repito cabizbajo
y vencido: hasta cuándo la cena durará.

Hay alguien que ha bebido mucho, y se burla,
y acerca y aleja de nosotros, como negra cuchara
de amarga esencia humana, la tumba …
                 Y menos sabe
ese oscuro hasta cuándo la cena durará!

## The Wretched Supper

How much longer are we to wait for what
is not our due ... And at which turn in the road shall we
straighten our poor knee for the last time! How much longer
          before
the cross urging us on lays down its oars.

How much longer will Doubt heap us with honors
for having suffered ...
                    We've been sitting
at the table for ages now, as bitter as a child
who, lying awake at midnight, weeps with hunger ...

And when will we meet the others, on the edge
of an eternal morning, all having breakfasted.
How much longer this vale of tears,
where I never asked to come.
                              Elbows on the table,
face bathed in tears, I repeat, head bowed
and defeated: how much longer will supper last.

Someone has drunk too much and keeps clowning around,
taunting us with the grave, dangling it before us, then
          snatching it away,
like a black spoonful of bitter human essence ...
                              And that obscure figure
has even less of an idea how long supper will last!

## Los dados eternos

Para Manuel González Prada, esta emoción
bravía y selecta, una de las que, con más
entusiasmo, me ha aplaudido el gran maestro.

Dios mío, estoy llorando el ser que vivo;
me pesa haber tomádote tu pan;
pero este pobre barro pensativo
no es costra fermentada en tu costado:
tú no tienes Marías que se van!

Dios mío, si tú hubieras sido hombre,
hoy supieras ser Dios;
pero tú, que estuviste siempre bien,
no sientes nada de tu creación.
Y el hombre sí te sufre: el Dios es él!

Hoy que en mis ojos brujos hay candelas,
como en un condenado,
Dios mío, prenderás todas tus velas,
y jugaremos con el viejo dado …
Tal vez ¡oh jugador! al dar la suerte
del universo todo,
surgirán las ojeras de la Muerte,
como dos ases fúnebres de lodo.

Dios mío y esta noche sorda, obscura,
ya no podrás jugar, porque la Tierra
es un dado roído y ya redondo

## The Eternal Dice

For Manuel González Prada, this rough-hewn,
rare emotion, one that the great master
applauded with most enthusiasm.*


My God, I'm weeping for my living being;
I regret having eaten your bread;
but this poor piece of thinking clay
is not a scab fermented in your side:
you have no Marys who will leave you!

My God, if you had ever been a man,
you'd know today how to be God;
but you, always so well-heeled,
feel nothing of what your creation feels.
And it's man who suffers you: *he* is the God!

Today, when there are candles in my witch eyes,
like one condemned to death,
you, my God, will light all your tapers,
and we'll play with the old dice ...
Perhaps, O gambler!, when you cast the die
for the fate of the whole universe,
the hollow eyes of Death will appear,
like two muddy, funereal dots.

My God, and on this dark, silent night
you won't be able to play, because the Earth
is a die worn round and smooth

----

* Prada (1844–1918) was a Peruvian poet, a literary critic, and the
director of the National Library of Peru. His views on literature and
on anarchist politics proved highly influential.

a fuerza de rodar a la aventura,
que no puede parar sino en un hueco,
en el hueco de inmensa sepultura.

from being rolled at random,
with its only stopping place a hole,
the hole of some vast tomb.

## Los anillos fatigados

Hay ganas de volver, de amar, de no ausentarse,
y hay ganas de morir, combatido por dos
aguas encontradas que jamás han de istmarse.

Hay ganas de un gran beso que amortaje a la Vida,
que acaba en el áfrica de una agonía ardiente, suicida!

Hay ganas de ... no tener ganas. Señor;
a ti yo te señalo con el dedo deicida;
hay ganas de no haber tenido corazón.

La primavera vuelve, vuelve y se irá. Y Dios,
curvado en tiempo, se repite, y pasa, pasa
a cuestas con la espina dorsal del Universo.

Cuando las sienes tocan su lúgubre tambor,
cuando me duele el sueño grabado en un puñal,
¡hay ganas de quedarse plantado en este verso!

## The Weary Rings

There's a desire to go back, to love, and not to leave,
a desire to die, fought over by two opposing
waters that will remain forever unisthmused.

A desire for an embrace so huge it would enshroud Life,
ending in the africa of a burning, suicidal agony!

A desire ... not to have desires, Lord;
and it's you I'm pointing at with this deicidal finger;
a desire never to have had a heart.

The spring returns, it returns and will leave. And God,
bent by time, comes again and passes, passes
with the spine of the Universe on his back.

When my temples beat their lugubrious drum,
when the dream, engraved on a dagger, pains me,
there's a desire to stay rooted here in this line of verse!

## Los pasos lejanos

Mi padre duerme. Su semblante augusto
figura un apacible corazón;
está ahora tan dulce ...
si hay algo en él de amargo, seré yo.

Hay soledad en el hogar; se reza;
y no hay noticias de los hijos hoy.
Mi padre se despierta, ausculta
la huida a Egipto, el restañante adiós.
Está ahora tan cerca;
si hay algo en él de lejos, seré yo.

Y mi madre pasea allá en los huertos,
saboreando un sabor ya sin sabor.
Está ahora tan suave,
tan ala, tan salida, tan amor.

Hay soledad en el hogar sin bulla,
sin noticias, sin verde, sin niñez.
Y si hay algo quebrado en esta tarde,
y que baja y que cruje,
son dos viejos caminos blancos, curvos.
Por ellos va mi corazón a pie.

## Distant Footsteps

My father sleeps. His august countenance
reveals a peaceful heart;
he's so sweet now ...
if there's any bitterness in him, it'll be me.

There's loneliness in the house; someone praying;
and no news of the children today.
My father wakes, he ponders
the flight into Egypt,* the still unhealed farewell.
He's so close now;
if there's any distance in him, it'll be me.

And my mother is out in the yard,
savoring a now savorless savor.
She's so gentle now,
so wing, so free, so love.

There's loneliness in the house without bustle,
without news, without greenness, without childhood.
And if there's anything broken this afternoon,
anything that bends and creaks,
it's two old white paths, curving away.
Along them goes my heart on foot.

———

* On a wall in Vallejo's childhood home, there was apparently a repro-
duction of a painting depicting this scene.

## A mi hermano Miguel

*In memoriam*

Hermano, hoy estoy en el poyo de la casa,
donde nos haces una falta sin fondo!
Me acuerdo que jugábamos esta hora, y que mamá
nos acariciaba: "Pero, hijos ..."

Ahora yo me escondo,
como antes, todas estas oraciones
vespertinas, y espero que tú no des conmigo.
Por la sala, el zaguán, los corredores.
Después, te ocultas tú, y yo no doy contigo.
Me acuerdo que nos hacíamos llorar,
hermano, en aquel juego.

Miguel, tú te escondiste
una noche de Agosto, al alborear;
pero, en vez de ocultarte riendo, estabas triste.
Y tu gemelo corazón de esas tardes
extintas se ha aburrido de no encontrarte. Y ya
cae sombra en el alma.

Oye, hermano, no tardes
en salir. Bueno? Puede inquietarse mamá.

## For My Brother Miguel

*In memoriam*

Brother, today, I'm sitting on the stone bench outside our house,
where you are so unendingly missed!
I remember that this was our time for playing together, and Mama
would say gently: "Now, boys ..."

Today I'm hiding,
as I used to do, every evening at
vespers, and I'm hoping you won't find me.
In the front room, the hallway, the corridors.
Then you hide, and I can't find you.
I remember how we made each other cry,
brother, playing that game.

Miguel, you hid yourself away
one August night as dawn was breaking;
but instead of laughing as you ran off to hide, you were sad.
And your heart-mate from those long-dead afternoons
has grown tired of not finding you. And
darkness has fallen on the soul.

Listen, brother, come out soon,
all right? Mama might get worried.

—————

Vallejo's brother, slightly older than him, died in 1915.

## Enereida

Mi padre, apenas,
en la mañana pajarina, pone
sus setentiocho años, sus setentiocho
ramos de invierno a solear.
El cementerio de Santiago, untado
en alegre año nuevo, está a la vista.
Cuántas veces sus pasos cortaron hacia él,
y tornaron de algún entierro humilde.

Hoy hace mucho tiempo que mi padre no sale!
Una broma de niños se desbanda.

Otras veces le hablaba a mi madre
de impresiones urbanas, de política;
y hoy, apoyado en su bastón ilustre
que sonara mejor en los años de la Gobernación,
mi padre está desconocido, frágil,
mi padre es una víspera.
Lleva, trae, abstraído, reliquias, cosas,
recuerdos, sugerencias.
La mañana apacible le acompaña
con sus alas blancas de hermana de la caridad.

## Enereid

My father, just barely,
in the bird-bright morning, puts
his seventy-eight years, his seventy-eight
winter branches, out in the sun.
The Santiago cemetery, anointed
with happy-new-yearness, is there before him.
How often his steps took the short cut through there,
and returned from some humble funeral.

My father hasn't left the house in ages now!
A cheerful band of children scatters.

Before, he used to talk to my mother
about town matters, about politics;
and now, leaning on his illustrious walking stick,[*]
which had a better ring to it when he was Governor,
my father is unrecognizable, frail,
my father is the eve of something.
He abstractedly carries to and fro relics, things,
memories, suggestions.
The calm morning accompanies him
with its sister-of-charity white wings.

———

The title is a neologism combining *enero* (January) and a reference to
the *Aeneid*. January is summer in Peru, and this poem is a celebration
of the seventy-eighth birthday of Vallejo's father.
[*] A reference to the ceremonial stick or mace used by Vallejo's father
when he was a governor in the district of Santiago de Chuco.

Día eterno es éste, día ingenuo, infante,
coral, oracional; se corona el tiempo de palomas,
y el futuro se puebla
de caravanas de inmortales rosas.
Padre, aún sigue todo despertando;
es Enero que canta, es tu amor
que resonando va en la Eternidad.
Aún reirás de tus pequeñuelos,
y habrá bulla triunfal en los Vacíos.

Aún será año nuevo. Habrá empanadas;
y yo tendré hambre, cuando toque a misa
en el beato campanario
el buen ciego mélico con quien
departieron mis sílabas escolares y frescas,
mi inocencia rotunda.
Y cuando la mañana llena de gracia,
desde sus senos de tiempo,
que son dos renuncias, dos avances de amor
que se tienden y ruegan infinito, eterna vida,
cante, y eche a volar Verbos plurales,
jirones de tu ser,
a la borda de sus alas blancas
de hermana de la caridad, ¡oh, padre mío!

This is an eternal day, an ingenuous, infant day,
choral, prayerful; time is crowned with doves,
and the future populated
with caravans of immortal roses.
Father, everything is still waking up;
it's January singing, it's your love
echoing through Eternity.
You'll still laugh at your little ones,
and there'll be a triumphal ruckus up in the Emptinesses.

It will still be new year. We'll have empanadas;
and I'll be hungry when summoned to mass
in the blessed bell tower
by the lyrical blind man* with whom,
in my rotund innocence,
I would chat away in my fresh, schoolboy syllables.
And when the morning full of grace—
from its breasts full of time,
which are two renunciations, two offers of love
reaching out and endlessly praying for eternal life—
sings and unleashes plural Verbs,
shreds of your being,
at the edges of its sister-of-charity
white wings, ah, then, my father!

* Santiago, the blind bell ringer at the local church that Vallejo at-
tended as a child.

## Espergesia

Yo nací un día
que Dios estuvo enfermo.

Todos saben que vivo,
que soy malo; y no saben
del Diciembre de ese Enero.
Pues yo nací un día
que Dios estuvo enfermo.

Hay un vacío
en mi aire metafísico
que nadie ha de palpar:
el claustro de un silencio
que habló a flor de fuego.

Yo nací un día
que Dios estuvo enfermo.

Hermano, escucha, escucha …
Bueno. Y que no me vaya
sin llevar diciembres,
sin dejar eneros.
Pues yo nací un día
que Dios estuvo enfermo.

## Espergesia

I was born on a day
when God was ill.

Everyone knows I'm alive,
that I'm bad; and they don't know
about the December of that January.
For I was born on a day
when God was ill.

There's an emptiness
in my metaphysical air
that no one will ever touch:
the cloistered silence
that spoke from the flames.

I was born on a day
when God was ill.

Brother, listen, listen ...
That's right. And don't let me leave
without taking Decembers with me,
without leaving Januarys behind.
For I was born on a day
when God was ill.

———

According to the Vallejo expert James Higgins, the title is "an archaic legal term, signifying the passing of a prison sentence. The poet explains his misery by the fact that Fate sentenced him to be born on a day when God was not up to the task of creation."

Todos saben que vivo,
que mastico ... Y no saben
por qué en mi verso chirrían,
oscuro sinsabor de féretro,
luyidos vientos
desenroscados de la Esfinge
preguntona del Desierto

Todos saben ... Y no saben
que la Luz es tísica,
y la Sombra gorda ...
Y no saben que el Misterio sintetiza ...
que él es la joroba
musical y triste que a distancia denuncia
el paso meridiano de las lindes a las Lindes.

Yo nací un día
que Dios estuvo enfermo,
grave.

Everyone knows I'm alive,
that I chew ... What they don't know
is why my verses creak,
dark coffin sorrow,
with chafing winds
unfurled by the busybody
Sphinx of the Desert.

Everyone knows ... What they don't know
is that the Light is consumptive,
and the Darkness obese ...
And they don't know that the mystery synthesizes ...
that it is the hump,
sad and musical, which, from afar, foretells
the meridian crossing from the borders to the Borders.

I was born on a day
when God was ill,
gravely.

## III

Las personas mayores
¿a qué hora volverán?
Da las seis el ciego Santiago,
y ya está muy oscuro.

Madre dijo que no demoraría.

Aguedita, Nativa, Miguel,
cuidado con ir por ahí, por donde
acaban de pasar gangueando sus memorias
dobladoras penas,
hacia el silencioso corral, y por donde
las gallinas que se están acostando todavía,
se han espantado tanto.
Mejor estemos aquí no más.
Madre dijo que no demoraría.

Ya no tengamos pena. Vamos viendo
los barcos ¡el mío es más bonito de todos!
con los cuales jugamos todo el santo día,
sin pelearnos, como debe de ser:
han quedado en el pozo de agua, listos,
fletados de dulces para mañana.

## III

The grown-ups
when will they come home? Blind Santiago
has just rung the six o'clock bell,
and it's already really dark.

Mama said she wouldn't be long.

Aguedita, Nativa,* Miguel,
watch out when you go down there,
some death-knell sorrows
have just passed by, clanging their memories,
heading straight for our silent yard,
where the chickens, alarmed by the noise,
have still not settled down for the night.
We'd best just stay here.
Mama said she wouldn't be long.

No need to be sad. Let's go and see
the boats—mine's the best!—
that we play with all day long,
no quarreling, of course:
they're on the pond, ready and waiting,
laden with candy for tomorrow.

————

Published 1922 in Lima, *Trilce* marked a major shift in style, full of
changes in register from formal to colloquial. The title is possibly a
fusion of *triste* (sad) and *dulce* (sweet).
* Aguedita and Nativa were two of Vallejo's sisters.

Aguardemos así, obedientes y sin más
remedio, la vuelta, el desagravio
de los mayores siempre delanteros
dejándonos en casa a los pequeños,
como si también nosotros
                              no pudiésemos partir.

Aguedita, Nativa, Miguel?
Llamo, busco al tanteo en la oscuridad.
No me vayan a haber dejado solo,
y el único recluso sea yo.

So let's wait obediently, what choice do we have,
for their return, and an apology
from the grown-ups who are always going off
and leaving the little ones at home,
as if we couldn't
                    leave too.

Aguedita, Nativa, Miguel?
I call, feeling around in the darkness.
Surely they haven't left me all alone,
and me the only prisoner.

# VI

El traje que vestí mañana
no lo ha lavado mi lavandera:
lo lavaba en sus venas otilinas,
en el chorro de su corazón, y hoy no he
de preguntarme si yo dejaba
el traje turbio de injusticia.

    A hora que no hay quien vaya a las aguas,
en mis falsillas encañona
el lienzo para emplumar, y todas las cosas
del velador de tánto qué será de mí,
todas no están mías
a mi lado.
Quedaron de su propiedad,
fratesadas, selladas con su trigueña bondad.

    Y si supiera si ha de volver;
y si supiera qué mañana entrará
a entregarme las ropas lavadas, mi aquella
lavandera del alma. Que mañana entrará

## VI

The suit I wore tomorrow
hasn't been washed by my laundress;
she used to wash it in her otiline veins,*
in the stream of her heart, and today I don't need
to ask myself if I left the suit
murky with injustice.

    Now there's no one to go and fetch water,
on my lined paper she irons
the linen into thick folds
ready to be feathered,† and all the things
on the night table of so many what'll-become-of-me's,
none of them are mine
here beside me.
They're her property now,
smoothed and sealed with her olive-skinned goodness.

    And if I knew she would come back;
and if I knew that tomorrow she would walk in
and hand me my laundered clothes, that laundress
of my soul. That tomorrow she would enter,

————

* A neologism referencing Vallejo's then lover, Otilia.
† This may refer to the ancient Peruvian art of feathering, covering
fabric panels with the brightly colored feathers of local birds, e.g.,
macaws. One critic also mentions that *emplumar* is Peruvian slang
for "run away."

satisfecha, capulí de obrería, dichosa
de probar que sí sabe, que sí puede
             ¡CÓMO NO VA A PODER!
azular y planchar todos los caos.

cherry-merry* with her handiwork, happy
to prove that she does know, that she really can
                   HOW COULD SHE NOT!
blue† and iron out all the chaoses.

---

* *Capulí* is a black cherry tree and its small, luscious fruit, and from
the context, I take it to mean here "proud" or "pleased," hence my
rather off-the-wall translation. According to the *OED*, *cherry-merry*
is an eighteenth-century term for "merry, esp. from conviviality."
† Since we're in laundry territory here, I take this to mean washing
or treating white clothes or linen with laundry blue.

## VII

Rumbé sin novedad por la veteada calle
que yo me sé. Todo sin novedad,
de veras. Y fondeé hacia cosas así,
y fui pasado.

Doblé la calle por la que raras
veces se pasa con bien, salida
heroica por la herida de aquella
esquina viva, nada a medias.

Son los grandores,
el grito aquel, la claridad de careo,
la barreta sumersa en su función de ¡ya!

Cuando la calle está ojerosa de puertas,
y pregona desde descalzos atriles
trasmañanar las salvas en los dobles.

Ahora hormigas minuteras
se adentran dulzoradas, dormitadas, apenas
dispuestas, y se baldan,
quemadas pólvoras, altos de a 1921.

## VII

I set off, as usual, down the veined street
I know so well. Nothing unusual about that,
nothing at all. And that's how I plumbed the depths,
and was—past tense.

I turned off down the street one rarely
walks down safely, a heroic
sortie through the wound of that
living corner, no half measures.

That's about the size of it,
the shout, the clarity of meeting face-to-face,
the plumb line submerged as a way of saying here now!

When the street is hollow-eyed with doors,
and preaches from discalced lecterns
postponing the salvos of death knells.

Now minute-hand ants
penetrate inside, sweetened, drowsy,
unprepared, and are squandered,
spent gunpowder, highs at 1921 prices!

## X

Prístina y última piedra de infundada
ventura, acaba de morir
con alma y todo, octubre habitación y encinta.
De tres meses de ausente y diez de dulce.
Cómo el destino,
mitrado monodáctilo, ríe.

Cómo detrás desahucian juntas
de contrarios. Cómo siempre asoma el guarismo
bajo la línea de todo avatar.

Cómo escotan las ballenas a palomas.
Cómo a su vez éstas dejan el pico
cubicado en tercera ala.
Cómo arzonamos, cara a monótonas ancas.

Se remolca diez meses hacia la decena,
hacia otro más allá.
Dos quedan por lo menos todavía en pañales.
Y los tres meses de ausencia.
Y los nueve de gestación.

## X

The final, pristine stone of a baseless
fortune has just died, soul and all,
pregnant October room.
Three months absence and ten of sweetness.*
How fate,
mitered monodactyl, laughs.

How, behind the scenes, whole juntas
of contraries are evicted. How the number always appears
beneath the line of every avatar.

How the whales trim the doves into shape.
How, in their turn, the latter rest their cubed beaks
under a third wing.
How we saddle up face-to-face with monotonous haunches.

Ten months hitch on to the next ten,
and another ten beyond.
Two at least remain in diapers.
And the three months of absence.
And the nine of gestation.

------

* This line and other references within the poem have been said to
refer to Vallejo's lover Otília's leaving him after he refused to marry
her, and when she may have already been pregnant. Vallejo, it seems,
never found out the truth of the matter.

No hay ni una violencia.
El paciente incorpórase,
y sentado empavona tranquilas misturas.

Not a hint of violence.
The patient sits up
and, still seated, anoints the air with calm confetti.[*]

---

[*] *Empavonar* can mean both to anoint and to frost glass, and *misturas* in Peru can mean confetti or scented flowers arranged on a tray to be carried in a procession. My translation is another example of imaginative guesswork.

## XI

He encontrado a una niña
en la calle, y me ha abrazado.
Equis, disertada, quien la halló y la halle,
no la va a recordar.

Esta niña es mi prima. Hoy, al tocarle
el talle, mis manos han entrado en su edad
como en par de mal rebocados sepulcros.
Y por la misma desolación marchóse,
              delta al sol tenebloso,
              trina entre los dos.

              "Me he casado",
me dice. Cuando lo que hicimos de niños
en casa de la tía difunta.
                    Se ha casado.
                    Se ha casado.

Tardes años latitudinales,
qué verdaderas ganas nos ha dado
de jugar a los toros, a las yuntas,
pero todo de engaños, de candor, como fue.

## XI

I met a girl
in the street, and she embraced me.
X declaring that whether you'd met her before or not,
you certainly wouldn't remember her.

This girl is my cousin. Today, when I touched
her waist, my hands entered her age
as if entering a pair of badly whitewashed tombs.
And because of that desolation she left,
                        delta in the tremebrous sun,
                        trine between the two of us.

                "I'm married,"
she tells me. When, as children, we used to play
in my late aunt's house.
                        She's married.
                        She's married.

Late latitudinal years,
how we loved to play
at bullfights, at leapfrog,
but all pretend, all innocent, as it was.

## XV

En el rincón aquel, donde dormimos juntos
tantas noches, ahora me he sentado
a caminar. La cuja de los novios difuntos
fue sacada, o talvez qué habrá pasado.

Has venido temprano a otros asuntos,
y ya no estás. Es el rincón
donde a tu lado, leí una noche,
entre tus tiernos puntos,
un cuento de Daudet. Es el rincón
amado. No lo equivoques.

Me he puesto a recordar los días
de verano idos, tu entrar y salir,
poca y harta y pálida por los cuartos.

En esta noche pluviosa,
ya lejos de ambos dos, salto de pronto ...
Son dos puertas abriéndose cerrándose,
dos puertas que al viento van y vienen
sombra          a          sombra.

## XV

In that corner, where we slept together
so many nights, I have just sat down
to go walking. The bed of the dead lovers
has been taken away, or who knows what happened?

    You came early to other matters,
and now you're not here. It's the corner
where, by your side, I read one night,
between your tender tips,
a story by Daudet. It's
the much-loved corner. You can't mistake it.

    I've been sitting here recalling the days
of summers past, your coming and going,
small and exhausted and pale, through the rooms.

    On this rainy night,
now far from both of us, I suddenly start ...
It's two doors opening closing,
two doors that come and go in the wind
shadow           to           shadow.

## XVIII

Oh las cuatro paredes de la celda.
Ah las cuatro paredes albicantes
que sin remedio dan al mismo número.

Criadero de nervios, mala brecha,
por sus cuatro rincones cómo arranca
las diarias aherrojadas extremidades.

Amorosa llavera de innumerables llaves,
si estuvieras aquí, si vieras hasta
qué hora son cuatro estas paredes.
Contra ellas seríamos contigo, los dos,
más dos que nunca. Y ni lloraras,
di, libertadora!

Ah las paredes de la celda.
De ellas me duelen entre tanto, más
las dos largas que tienen esta noche
algo de madres que ya muertas
llevan por bromurados declives,
a un niño de la mano cada una.

Y sólo yo me voy quedando,
con la diestra, que hace por ambas manos,
en alto, en busca de terciario brazo
que ha de pupilar, entre mi donde y mi cuando,
esta mayoría inválida de hombre.

## XVIII

Oh, the four walls of this cell.
Ah, the four whitewashed walls
that always come to the same number.

Breeding ground of nerves, vile place,
how from its four corners it drags up
the day's shackled extremities.

Loving keeper of innumerable keys,*
if you were here, if you could see for how
long these walls remain four.
With you here, we would be two against four,
more two than ever. And you wouldn't even cry,
would you, my liberator!

Ah, the walls of this cell.
The ones that hurt me most, though,
are the two long walls, which tonight have something
about them of mothers already dead,
each leading by the hand,
down bromidic slopes, a young child.

And only I remain here,
with my right hand, which serves for both,
raised, in search of a tertiary arm
to keep watch, between my where and my when,
over this invalid manhood.

————

* A reference to Vallejo's mother, who died in 1918 but came to
represent to the poet all that was positive in life.

## XXVIII

He almorzado solo ahora, y no he tenido
madre, ni súplica, ni sírvete, ni agua,
ni padre que, en el facundo ofertorio
de los choclos, pregunte para su tardanza
de imagen, por los broches mayores del sonido.

Cómo iba yo a almorzar. Cómo me iba a servir
de tales platos distantes esas cosas,
cuando habráse quebrado el propio hogar,
cuando no asoma ni madre a los labios.
Çómo iba yo a almorzar nonada.

A la mesa de un buen amigo he almorzado
con su padre recién llegado del mundo,
con sus canas tías que hablan
en tordillo retinte de porcelana,
bisbiseando por todos sus viudos alvéolos;
y con cubiertos francos de alegres tiroriros,
porque estánse en su casa. Así, qué gracia!
Y me han dolido los cuchillos
de esta mesa en todo el paladar.

El yantar de estas mesas así, en que se prueba
amor ajeno en vez del propio amor,

## XXVIII

I've just lunched alone,* with no
mother, no could-you-pass-me, no help-yourself, no water,
no father who, during the eloquent offertory
of corn on the cob, might inquire about your late
appearance, above the louder clasps of sound.

How could I possibly eat. How help myself
to those things from those distant plates,
when my own home was broken,
when not even mother is on anyone's lips.
How was I going to eat anything at all.

At a good friend's table I lunched
with his father newly arrived from the world,
with his gray-haired aunts who speak
in a dappled porcelain tinkle
lisping through their widowed teeth;
and with the cutlery tootling merrily away,
because they're at home. How lovely!
And yet the knives on that table
made my whole palate ache.

Dining at such tables, where one feels
other people's love instead of one's own,

———

* According to his biographer Juan Espejo Asturrizaga, Vallejo had
been invited to have lunch at the home of Espejo's aunts, along with
Espejo's father. Vallejo, however, arrived late and ended up eating
lunch alone.

torna tierra el bocado que no brinda la
               MADRE,
hace golpe la dura deglusión; el dulce,
hiel; aceite funéreo, el café.
Cuando ya se ha quebrado el propio hogar,
y el sírvete materno no sale de la
tumba,
la cocina a oscuras, la miseria de amor.

turns to earth the mouthful not served by
MOTHER,
makes a blow out of each hard gulp; dessert,
bile; coffee, funereal oil.
When your own home's been broken,
and no maternal do-help-yourself emerges from
the grave,
the kitchen in darkness, the misery of love.

## XXXV

El encuentro con la amada
tánto alguna vez, es un simple detalle,
casi un programa hípico en violado,
que de tan largo no se puede doblar bien.

El almuerzo con ella que estaría
poniendo el plato que nos gustara ayer
y se repite ahora,
pero con algo más de mostaza;
el tenedor absorto, su doneo radiante
de pistilo en mayo, y su verecundia
de a centavito, por quítame allá esa paja.
Y la cerveza lírica y nerviosa
a la que celan sus dos pezones sin lúpulo,
y que no se debe tomar mucho!

Y los demás encantos de la mesa
que aquella núbil campaña borda
con sus propias baterías germinales
que han operado toda la mañana,
según me consta, a mí,
amoroso notario de sus intimidades,
y con las diez varillas mágicas
de sus dedos pancreáticos.

Mujer que, sin pensar en nada más allá,
suelta el mirlo y se pone a conversarnos
sus palabras tiernas
como lancinantes lechugas recién cortadas.

## XXXV

The encounter with the beloved
is often a simple detail,
a violet-colored race card
too large to fold up easily.

Lunch with her, who would be
serving the dish we'd enjoyed yesterday
and are having again today,
but with a little more mustard;
her fork absorbed, her radiant coquetry,
that of a pistil in May, and her penny piece
blushes about the tiniest thing.
And the lyrical, nervous beer,
watched over by her two hop-free nipples:
now, don't drink too much!

And the other delights of the table
which that nubile campaign embroiders
with her own germinal artillery
which has been firing all morning,
as I understand it, I,
the amorous notary of her most intimate parts,
as well as the ten magic wands
of her pancreatic fingers.

The woman who, without so much as a thought,
starts chattering, and begins talking to us,
her words tender
as crisp, fresh-cut lettuces.

Otro vaso, y me voy. Y nos marchamos,
ahora sí, a trabajar.

Entre tanto, ella se interna
entre los cortinajes y ¡oh aguja de mis días
desgarrados! se sienta a la orilla
de una costura, a coserme el costado
a su costado,
a pegar el botón de esa camisa,
que se ha vuelto a caer. Pero hase visto!

One more glass, and I'm off. And now we really do leave,
to go to work.

Meanwhile, she installs herself
in between the curtains, and then she, O, needle of my
torn and brazen days!, sits down at the edge
of a seam, stitching my ribs
to her ribs,
sewing on the shirt button
that has fallen off again. Can you believe it!

## XLV

Me desvinculo del mar
cuando vienen las aguas a mí.

Salgamos siempre. Saboreemos
la canción estupenda, la canción dicha
por los labios inferiores del deseo.
Oh prodigiosa doncellez.
Pasa la brisa sin sal.

A lo lejos husmeo los tuétanos
oyendo el tanteo profundo, a la caza
de teclas de resaca.

Y si así diéramos las narices
en el absurdo,
nos cubriremos con el oro de no tener nada,
y empollaremos el ala aún no nacida
de la noche, hermana
de esta ala huérfana del día,
que a fuerza de ser una ya no es ala.

*XLV*

I unlink myself from the sea
when the waters come to me.

Let's go then. Let's savor
the stupendous song, the song sung
by the lower lips of desire.
O prodigious maidenhood.
The saltless wind passes by.

In the distance I can sniff out the essence,
hear the searching touch, on the hunt
for the keys of the undertow.

And if we then walk smack
into the absurd,
we'll cover ourselves with the gold-of-having-nothing,
and will hatch out the as-yet-unborn wing
of night, sister
of this orphaned wing of day,
which, being one, is no longer a wing.

## LVI

Todos los días amanezco a ciegas
a trabajar para vivir; y tomo el desayuno,
sin probar ni gota de él, todas las mañanas.
Sin saber si he logrado, o más nunca,
algo que brinca del sabor
o es sólo corazón y que ya vuelto, lamentará
hasta dónde esto es lo menos.

El niño crecería ahito de felicidad
                              oh albas,
ante el pesar de los padres de no poder dejarnos
de arrancar de sus sueños de amor a este mundo;
ante ellos que, como Dios, de tanto amor
se comprendieron hasta creadores
y nos quisieron hasta hacernos daño.

Flecos de invisible trama,
dientes que huronean desde la neutra emoción,
                              pilares
libres de base y coronación,
en la gran boca que ha perdido el habla.

Fósforo y fósforo en la oscuridad,
lágrima y lágrima en la polvareda.

## LVI

Every day I wake blindly
to go and work for a living, and I eat breakfast
without tasting a thing, every morning.
Never knowing if I have achieved, or ever will,
something that bursts with flavor,
or is only heart, which, once it returns, will think
regretfully, oh, was that all it was.

The child will grow up sated with happiness,
                               O dawns,
faced by our parents' sadness not to allow us
to escape from their dreams of love into this world;
faced by them, who, like God, out of so much love
believed themselves to be our creators,
and loved us so much they hurt us.

Frayed fringes of an invisible weft,
teeth ferreting out from some neutral emotion,
                               pillars
without base or capital,
in the vast mouth that has lost the power of speech.

Match after match in the darkness,
tear after tear in the dust.

## LXI

Esta noche desciendo del caballo,
ante la puerta de la casa, donde
me despedí con el cantar del gallo.
Está cerrada y nadie responde.

El poyo en que mamá alumbró
al hermano mayor, para que ensille
lomos que había yo montado en pelo,
por rúas y por cercas, niño aldeano;
el poyo en que dejé que se amarille al sol
mi adolorida infancia ... ¿Y este duelo
que enmarca la portada?

Dios en la paz foránea,
estornuda, cual llamando también, el bruto;
husmea, golpeando el empedrado. Luego duda,
relincha,
orejea a viva oreja.

Ha de velar papá rezando, y quizás
pensará se me hizo tarde.
Las hermanas, canturreando sus ilusiones
sencillas, bullosas,
en la labor para la fiesta que se acerca,
y ya no falta casi nada.
Espero, espero, el corazón

## LXI

Tonight I get off my horse
at the door of the house where once
I took my leave at cockcrow.
It's all shut up, and no one answers.

The stone bench where Mama gave light*
to my older brother, so he could saddle
backs I rode bareback,
along lanes and past hedges, a country boy;
the bench where I left my grieving childhood
yellowing in the sun … And this black grief
framing the doorway?

God in this strange peace,
the animal sneezes, as if he, too, were calling;
he snuffles, pawing the cobbles. Then hesitates,
neighs,
eavesdropping, all ears.

Papa must be awake, praying, thinking
perhaps I've been delayed.
My sisters humming along to their
simple hopes, bustling about,
making ready for the coming fiesta,
so close it's almost here.
I wait, I wait, my heart

---

* *Alumbrar* means to shed light on something, but also to give birth.
My translation attempts to have it both ways.

un huevo en su momento, que se obstruye.
Numerosa familia que dejamos
no ha mucho, hoy nadie en vela, y ni una cera
puso en el ara para que volviéramos.

Llamo de nuevo, y nada.
Callamos y nos ponemos a sollozar, y el animal
relincha, relincha más todavía.

Todos están durmiendo para siempre,
y tan de lo más bien, que por fin
mi caballo acaba fatigado por cabecear
a su vez, y entre sueños, a cada venia, dice
que está bien, que todo está muy bien.

an egg about to hatch, that stops.
Of the large family we left
not long ago, today no one's awake and watching,
no one placed a candle on the altar for our return.

I knock again, and nothing.
We fall silent and begin to sob, and the horse
Neighs, neighs even more.

All are eternally asleep,
and so soundly that, in the end, my horse
grows weary and, in turn, nods off,
and in between dreams, with each nod of his head, he says:
it's fine, everything's fine.

## LXXVII

Graniza tánto, como para que yo recuerde
y acreciente las perlas
que he recogido del hocico mismo
de cada tempestad.

No se vaya a secar esta lluvia.
A menos que me fuese dado
caer ahora para ella, o que me enterrasen
mojado en el agua
que surtiera de todos los fuegos.

¿Hasta dónde me alcanzará esta lluvia?
Temo me quede con algún flanco seco;
temo que ella se vaya, sin haberme probado
en las sequías de increíbles cuerdas vocales,
por las que,
para dar armonía,
hay siempre que subir ¡nunca bajar!
¿No subimos acaso para abajo?

Canta, lluvia, en la costa aún sin mar!

## LXXVII

It's hailing so hard, as if to remind me
and add to the pearls
I've gathered from the snout
of every storm.

Don't let this rain ever stop.
Unless it were given to me
to fall instead or to be buried
drenched in the water
spouting forth from all the fires.

How deeply will it soak me through, this rain?
I'm afraid I might be left with one dry flank;
I'm afraid it will stop, leaving me untested
in the dry spells of incredible vocal cords,
according to which,
to create harmony,
you always have to go up, never down!
Or do we perhaps always go up downwards?

Sing, rain, on this coast that still has no sea!

## La violencia de las horas

Todos han muerto.

Murió doña Antonia, la ronca, que hacía pan barato en el burgo.

Murió el cura Santiago, a quien placía le saludasen los jóvenes y las mozas, respondiéndoles a todos, indistintamente: "Buenos días, José! Buenos días, María!"

Murió aquella joven rubia, Carlota, dejando un hijito de meses, que luego también murió a los ocho días de la madre.

Murió mi tía Albina, que solía cantar tiempos y modos de heredad, en tanto cosía en los corredores, para Isidora, la criada de oficio, la honrosísima mujer.

Murió un viejo tuerto, su nombre no recuerdo, pero dormía al sol de la mañana, sentado ante la puerta del hojalatero de la esquina.

Murió Rayo, el perro de mi altura, herido de un balazo de no se sabe quién.

*from* Poems in Prose

## The Violence of the Hours

They've all died.

Doña Antonia died, the one with the gruff voice, who used to bake cheap bread in the village.

Santiago the priest died, he was always so pleased when the young men and women would greet him, and he would respond to them all regardless: "Good morning, José!" or "Good morning, María!"

That fair-haired young woman, Carlota, died, leaving a little boy only a few months old, who also died, eight days after his mother.

My aunt Albina died, she used to sit in the corridor sewing and singing inherited tempos and modes for Isidora, her official maid, that very honorable woman.

A one-eyed old man died, I don't remember his name, but he used to fall asleep in the morning sunshine, sitting outside the tinsmith's shop on the corner.

My dog Lightning died, he was almost as tall as me, killed by a bullet from who knows who.

———

These poems were written between 1923 and 1927, when Vallejo was already living in Paris, and show his growing political commitment.

Murió Lucas, mi cuñado en la paz de las cinturas, de quien me acuerdo cuando llueve y no hay nadie en mi experiencia.

Murió en mi revólver mi madre, en mi puño mi hermana y mi hermano en mi víscera sangrienta, los tres ligados por un género triste de tristeza, en el mes de agosto de años sucesivos.

Murió el músico Méndez, alto y muy borracho, que solfeaba en su clarinete tocatas melancólicas, a cuyo articulado se dormían las gallinas de mi barrio, mucho antes de que el sol se fuese.

Murió mi eternidad y estoy velándola.

Lucas, my brother-in-law, died peacefully and at home, I think of him whenever it rains and there's no one else to share the experience.

My mother died in my revolver, my sister in my fist and my brother in my bloody innards, all three connected by a sad kind of sadness, on consecutive Augusts.

Méndez the musician died, tall and very drunk, and who would sol-fa melancholy toccatas on his clarinet, at whose sounds the chickens in my neighborhood would fall asleep, long before the sun had set.

My eternity died and here I am keeping vigil.

## El momento más grave de la vida

Un hombre dijo:

—El momento más grave de mi vida estuvo en la batalla del Marne, cuando fui herido en el pecho.

Otro hombre dijo:

—El momento más grave de mi vida, ocurrió en un maremoto de Yokohama, del cual salvé milagrosamente, refugiado bajo el alero de una tienda de lacas.

Y otro hombre dijo:

—El momento más grave de mi vida acontece cuando duermo de día.

Y otro dijo:

—El momento más grave de mi vida ha estado en mi mayor soledad.

Y otro dijo:

—El momento más grave de mi vida fue mi prisión en una cárcel del Perú.

Y otro dijo:

## The Worst Moment in Life

A man said:

"The worst moment in my life was during the battle of the Marne, when I was wounded in the chest."

Another man said:

"The worst moment in my life was in a seaquake in Yokohama, which, miraculously, I survived, sheltering under the eaves of a lacquerware shop."

And another man said:

"The worst moment in my life is when I fall asleep in the daytime."

And another said:

"The worst moment in my life was when I was at my loneliest."

And another said:

"The worst moment in my life was being locked up in Peru."

And another said:

—El momento más grave de mi vida es el haber sorprendido de perfil a mi padre.

Y el ultimo hombre dijo:

—El momento más grave de mi vida no ha llegado todavía.

"The worst moment in my life was catching my father in profile."

And the last man said:

"The worst moment in my life hasn't yet arrived."

## Voy a hablar de la esperanza

Yo no sufro este dolor como César Vallejo. Yo no me duelo ahora como artista, como hombre ni como simple ser vivo siquiera. Yo no sufro este dolor como católico, como mahometano ni como ateo. Hoy sufro solamente. Si no me llamase César Vallejo, también sufriría este mismo dolor. Si no fuese artista, también lo sufriría. Si no fuese hombre ni ser vivo siquiera, también lo sufriría. Si no fuese católico, ateo ni mahometano, también lo sufriría. Hoy sufro desde más abajo. Hoy sufro solamente.

Me duelo ahora sin explicaciones. Mi dolor es tan hondo, que no tuvo ya causa ni carece de causa. ¿Qué sería su causa? ¿Dónde está aquello tan importante, que dejase de ser su causa? Nada es su causa; nada ha podido dejar de ser su causa. ¿A qué ha nacido este dolor, por sí mismo? Mi dolor es del viento del norte y del viento del sur, como esos huevos neutros que algunas aves raras ponen del viento. Si hubiera muerto mi novia, mi dolor sería igual. Si me hubieran cortado el cuello de raíz, mi dolor sería igual. Si la vida fuese, en fin, de otro modo, mi dolor sería igual. Hoy sufro desde más arriba. Hoy sufro solamente.

Miro el dolor del hambriento y veo que su hambre anda tan lejos de mi sufrimiento, que de quedarme ayuno hasta morir, saldría siempre de mi tumba una brizna de yerba al menos. Lo mismo el enamorado. ¡Qué sangre la suya más engendrada, para la mía sin fuente ni consumo!

## I'm Going to Talk about Hope

I do not feel this pain as César Vallejo. I do not suffer now as an artist, as a man, or even as a simple living being. I don't feel this pain as a Catholic, as a Muslim, or as an atheist. Today I simply suffer. And I would feel the same pain even if my name wasn't César Vallejo. I would feel it even if I wasn't an artist. I would suffer even if I wasn't a man or a living being. I would suffer even if I wasn't a Catholic, an atheist, or a Muslim. Today my suffering comes from somewhere deeper down. Today I simply suffer.

I hurt now for no explicable reason. My pain is so deep that it has neither cause nor absence of cause. What could that cause be? What could possibly be so important that it would cease to be its cause? Nothing is its cause; nothing has ceased to be its cause. What is the purpose of this pain, born of itself? My pain is the wind from the north and the wind from the south, like those sterile eggs that some rare birds lay on the wind. If my girlfriend had died, my pain would be the same. If they had slit my throat, my pain would be the same. If life were, let's say, different, my pain would be the same. Today I am suffering from higher up. Today I simply suffer.

I see the pain of the starving and I see how far their hunger is from my suffering, that even if I fasted to death, there would always be one blade of grass growing on my grave. The same goes for lovers. Their blood has progenitors, whereas mine has no provenance and no purpose!

Yo creía hasta ahora que todas las cosas del universo eran, inevitablemente, padres o hijos. Pero he aquí que mi dolor de hoy no es padre ni es hijo. Le falta espalda para anochecer, tanto como le sobra pecho para amanecer y si lo pusiesen en la estancia oscura, no daría luz y si lo pusiesen en una estancia luminosa, no echaría sombra. Hoy sufro suceda lo que suceda. Hoy sufro solamente.

Up until now, I believed that all the things in the universe were, inevitably, parents or children. But here I am, and today's pain is neither parent nor child. It lacks sufficient backbone to grow dark and is too arrogant to grow light, and if they were to put it in a dark room, it wouldn't give off any light, and if they were to put it in a well-lit room, it would cast no shadow. Today I suffer regardless of what happens. Today I simply suffer.

## Hallazgo de la vida

¡Señores! Hoy es la primera vez que me doy cuenta de la presencia de la vida. ¡Señores! Ruego a ustedes dejarme libre un momento, para saborear esta emoción formidable, espontánea y reciente de la vida, que hoy, por la primera vez, me extasía y me hace dichoso hasta las lágrimas.

Mi gozo viene de lo inédito de mi emoción. Mi exultación viene de que antes no sentí la presencia de la vida. No la he sentido nunca. Miente quien diga que la he sentido. Miente y su mentira me hiere a tal punto que me haría desgraciado. Mi gozo viene de mi fe en este hallazgo personal de la vida, y nadie puede ir contra esta fe. Al que fuera, se le caería la lengua, se le caerían los huesos y correría el peligro de recoger otros, ajenos, para mantenerse de pie ante mis ojos.

Nunca, sino ahora, ha habido vida. Nunca, sino ahora, han pasado gentes. Nunca, sino ahora, ha habido casas y avenidas, aire y horizonte. Si viniese ahora mi amigo Peyriet, les diría que yo no le conozco y que debemos empezar de nuevo. ¿Cuándo, en efecto, le he conocido a mi amigo Peyriet? Hoy sería la primera vez que nos conocemos. Le diría que se vaya y regrese y entre a verme, como si no me conociera, es decir, por la primera vez.

## The Discovery of Life

Gentlemen! Today is the first time I've become aware of the presence of life. Gentlemen! I ask you to leave me alone for a moment so that I may savor this formidable, spontaneous, and utterly new emotion of life, which, today, for the first time, thrills me and makes me so happy I could cry.

My pleasure derives from the unprecedented nature of this emotion. This exultation comes from my never before having felt the presence of life. Never. Anyone who says they have is lying. They are lying, and their lie wounds me so deeply it would grieve me. My pleasure comes from my faith in this personal discovery of life, and no one can deny that faith. If anyone did, their tongue would fall out, their bones would fall out, and they would run the risk of having to pick up other people's bones so as to remain standing before me.

Never, until now, has life existed. Never, until now, have people walked past. Never, until now, have there been houses and avenues, air and horizon. If my friend Peyriet were to come to me now, I would tell him that I don't know him, and that we will have to start again. I mean, when *did* I meet my friend Peyriet? This would be the first time we have met. I would tell him to go out and come back in as if he didn't know me, that is, as if we were meeting for the first time.

Ahora yo no conozco a nadie ni nada. Me advierto en un país extraño, en el que todo cobra relieve de nacimiento, luz de epifanía inmarcesible. No, señor. No hable usted a ese caballero. Usted no lo conoce y le sorprendería tan inopinada parla. No ponga usted el pie sobre esa piedrecilla: quién sabe no es piedra y vaya usted a dar en el vacío. Sea usted precavido, puesto que estamos en un mundo absolutamente inconocido.

¡Cuán poco tiempo he vivido! Mi nacimiento es tan reciente, que no hay unidad de medida para contar mi edad. ¡Si acabo de nacer! ¡Si aún no he vivido todavía! Señores: soy tan pequeñito, que el día apenas cabe en mí.

Nunca, sino ahora, oí el estruendo de los carros, que cargan piedras para una gran construcción del boulevard Haussmann. Nunca, sino ahora avancé paralelamente a la primavera, diciéndola: "Si la muerte hubiera sido otra ..." Nunca, sino ahora, vi la luz áurea del sol sobre las cúpulas de Sacré-Coeur. Nunca, sino ahora, se me acercó un niño y me miró hondamente con su boca. Nunca, sino ahora, supe que existía una puerta, otra puerta y el canto cordial de las distancias.

¡Dejadme! La vida me ha dado ahora en toda mi muerte.

Today I don't know anyone or anything. I find myself in a strange land, in which everything appears as if newborn, the light of an imperishable epiphany. No, sir. Don't speak to that gentleman. You don't know him, and he would be taken aback were you to suddenly address him. Don't step on that stone over there; who knows, it might not be a stone and you might step into the void. Be very cautious, because we are in a completely unknown world.

How short a time I have lived! My birth is so recent that no existing unit of measurement could possibly calculate my age. I have only just been born! I haven't even lived yet! Gentlemen: I'm so tiny that even the day is too large for me.

Never, until now, have I heard the noise of carts transporting stones to begin the major project of building Boulevard Haussmann. Never, until now, have I walked in parallel with the spring, saying: "If only death had been different..." Never, until now, have I seen the golden light of the sun on the cupolas of the Sacré-Coeur. Never, until now, has a child come up to me and looked at me deeply with his mouth. Never, until now, did I know that there was a door, another door, and the cordial song of distances.

Leave me! Life has just struck me now in all my death.

## No vive ya nadie...

—No vive ya nadie en la casa—me dices—; todos se han ido. La sala, el dormitorio, el patio, yacen despoblados. Nadie ya queda, pues que todos han partido.

Y yo te digo: Cuando alguien se va, alguien queda. El punto por donde pasó un hombre, ya no está solo. Únicamente está solo, de soledad humana, el lugar por donde ningún hombre ha pasado. Las casas nuevas están más muertas que las viejas, porque sus muros son de piedra o de acero, pero no de hombres. Una casa viene al mundo, no cuando la acaban de edificar, sino cuando empiezan a habitarla. Una casa vive únicamente de hombres, como una tumba. De aquí esa irresistible semejanza que hay entre una casa y una tumba. Sólo que la casa se nutre de la vida del hombre, mientras que la tumba se nutre de la muerte del hombre. Por eso la primera está de pie, mientras que la segunda está tendida.

Todos han partido de la casa, en realidad, pero todos se han quedado en verdad. Y no es el recuerdo de ellos lo que queda, sino ellos mismos. Y no es tampoco que ellos queden en la casa, sino que continúan por la casa. Las funciones y los actos se van de la casa en tren o en avión o a caballo, a pie o arrastrándose. Lo que continúa en la casa es el órgano, el agente en gerundio y en círculo. Los pasos se han ido, los besos, los perdones, los crímenes. Lo que continúa en la casa es el pie, los labios, los ojos, el corazón. Las negaciones y las afirmaciones, el bien y el mal, se han dispersado. Lo que continúa en la casa, es el sujeto del acto.

## "No one lives there anymore..."

"No one lives in the house anymore," you tell me; "they've all gone. The living room, the bedroom, the yard, are all deserted. No one is left, because they've all gone away."

And I tell you: "When someone leaves, someone stays behind. No place where man has set foot can ever be said to be alone. Only a place where no one has ever been can be said to be alone with a human loneliness. New houses are more dead than old ones, because their walls are made of stone or steel but not of people. A house comes into the world, not when it has finished being built, but when it begins to be inhabited. A house lives solely on people, like a grave. That's why there is such an irresistible similarity between a house and a grave, except that the house feeds off a person's life, while the grave feeds off their death. That's why the former stands upright while the latter lies down."

Everyone really has left the house, but they have also all stayed behind. And it isn't the memory of them that remains, but they themselves. And it isn't that they're still physically there in the house, but that they continue to walk around in it. All the functions and actions leave the house by train or by plane or by horse, or on foot or crawling. What continues in the house is the organ, the agent in the form of gerund and circle. The footsteps have gone, so have the kisses, the apologies, the crimes. What continues in the house are the foot, the lips, the eyes, the heart. The denials and affirmations, the good and the bad, have all dispersed. What continues in the house is the subject of the act."

## Altura y pelos

¿Quién no tiene su vestido azul?
¿Quién no almuerza y no toma el tranvía,
con su cigarrillo contratado y su dolor de bolsillo?
¡Yo que tan sólo he nacido!
¡Yo que tan sólo he nacido!

¿Quién no escribe una carta?
¿Quién no habla de un asunto muy importante,
muriendo de costumbre y llorando de oído?
¡Yo que solamente he nacido!
¡Yo que solamente he nacido!

¿Quién no se llama Carlos o cualquier otra cosa?
¿Quién al gato no dice gato gato?
¡Ay, yo que sólo he nacido solamente!
¡Ay!, yo que sólo he nacido solamente!

## Height and Hairs

Who doesn't own a blue suit?
Who doesn't have lunch and take the tram,
with his statutory cigarette and pocket-sized pain?
Me, and all I did was to be born!
Me, and all I did was to be born!

Who doesn't write a letter?
Who doesn't speak of a very important matter,
dying out of sheer habit and weeping solely by ear?
Me, and I was simply born!
Me, and I was simply born!

Who isn't called Carlos or some other name?
Who doesn't say to the cat, pussy cat pussy cat?
Me, and all I did was simply to be born!
Me, and all I did was simply to be born!

———

We have no accurate dates for when Vallejo wrote these poems, but it
was probably between the late 1920s and mid-1936. Nor do we know
if he had finished revising the poems or if this would have been his
chosen title for the book, which was published posthumously by his
widow, Georgette Vallejo.

## Los desgraciados

Ya va a venir el día; da
cuerda a tu brazo, búscate debajo
del colchón, vuelve a pararte
en tu cabeza, para andar derecho.
Ya va a venir el día, ponte el saco.

Ya va a venir el día; ten
fuerte en la mano a tu intestino grande, reflexiona,
antes de meditar, pues es horrible
cuando le cae a uno la desgracia
y se le cae a uno a fondo el diente.

Necesitas comer, pero, me digo,
no tengas pena, que no es de pobres
la pena, el sollozar junto a su tumba;
remiéndate, recuerda,
confía en tu hilo blanco, fuma, pasa lista
a tu cadena y guárdala detrás de tu retrato.
Ya va a venir el día, ponte el alma.

Ya va a venir el día; pasan,
han abierto en el hotel un ojo,
azotándolo, dándole con un espejo tuyo . . .
¿Tiemblas? Es el estado remoto de la frente
y la nación reciente del estómago.
Roncan aún . . . ¡Qué universo se lleva este ronquido!
¡Cómo quedan tus poros, enjuiciándolo!

## The Unfortunates

The day is about to come;
wind up your arm, look for yourself under
the mattress, go back to standing
on your head so that you can walk straight.
The day is about to come, put on your jacket.

The day is about to come; keep
a firm hold on your large intestine, reflect
rather than meditate, because it's horrible
when misfortune falls on you
and your tooth falls deep inside you.

You need to eat, but, I tell myself,
don't grieve, grief isn't
for the poor, nor is sobbing over someone's grave;
patch yourself up, remember,
trust in your white thread, smoke, do a roll call
of your chains and stow it behind your portrait.
The day is about to come, so put on your soul.

The day is about to come; they pass,
they've opened an eye in the hotel,
whipping it, beating it with one of your mirrors …
Are you trembling? It's the remote state of your forehead
and the recent nation of your stomach.
They're still snoring … What a universe that snore carries
                within it!
And just look at your pores, passing judgment on it!

¡Con cuántos doses ¡ay! estás tan solo!
Ya va a venir el día, ponte el sueño.

Ya va a venir el día, repito
por el órgano oral de tu silencio
y urge tomar la izquierda con el hambre
y tomar la derecha con la sed; de todos modos,
abstente de ser pobre con los ricos,
atiza
tu frío, porque en él se integra mi calor, amada víctima.
Ya va a venir el día, ponte el cuerpo.

Ya va a venir el día;
la mañana, la mar, el meteoro, van
en pos de tu cansancio, con banderas,
y, por tu orgullo clásico, las hienas
cuentan sus pasos al compás del asno,
la panadera piensa en ti,
el carnicero piensa en ti, palpando
el hacha en que están presos
el acero y el hierro y el metal; jamás olvides
que durante la misa no hay amigos.
Ya va a venir el día, ponte el sol.

Ya viene el día; dobla
el aliento, triplica
tu bondad rencorosa
y da codos al miedo, nexo y énfasis,
pues tú, como se observa en tu entrepierna y siendo
el malo ¡ay! inmortal,
has soñado esta noche que vivías
de nada y morías de todo ...

Even with all those twos, you're so alone.
The day is about to come, put on a dream.

The day is about to come, I repeat
through the oral organ of your silence,
and you must take the left turn with your hunger
and the right with your thirst; at any rate,
refrain from being poor with the rich,
stoke up
your coldness, because my heat is a part of it, beloved victim.
The day is about to come, put on your body.

The day is about to come;
the morning, the sea, the meteor, all
are in hot pursuit of your tiredness, flags flying,
and because of your classic pride, the hyenas
count their steps at donkey pace,
the baker, she's thinking about you,
the butcher's thinking about you, stroking
his cleaver in which lie imprisoned
steel and iron and metal; never forget
that during mass there are no friends.
The day is about to come, put on the sun.

The day is coming; double
your breath, triple
your rancorous kindness,
and elbow aside fear, connection, and emphasis,
for you, as one can see from your crotch and given
that evil is, alas, immortal,
you dreamed last night that you were living
on nothing and dying of everything ...

## Los nueve monstruos

Y, desgraciadamente,
el dolor crece en el mundo a cada rato,
crece a treinta minutos por segundo, paso a paso,
y la naturaleza del dolor, es el dolor dos veces
y la condición del martirio, carnívora, voraz,
es el dolor dos veces
y la función de la yerba purísima, el dolor
dos veces
y el bien de sér, dolernos doblemente.

Jamás, hombres humanos,
hubo tánto dolor en el pecho, en la solapa, en la cartera,
en el vaso, en la carnicería, en la aritmética!
Jamás tánto cariño doloroso,
jamás tánta cerca arremetió lo lejos,
jamás el fuego nunca
jugó mejor su rol de frío muerto!
Jamás, señor ministro de salud, fue la salud
más mortal
y la migraña extrajo tanta frente de la frente!
Y el mueble tuvo en su cajón, dolor,
el corazón, en su cajón, dolor,
la lagartija, en su cajón, dolor.

Crece la desdicha, hermanos hombres,
más pronto que la máquina, a diez máquinas, y crece
con la res de Rousseau, con nuestras barbas;

## The Nine Monsters

And, unfortunately,
pain is growing in the world all the time,
it grows at thirty minutes per second, step by step,
and the nature of the pain is pain twice over,
and the condition of martyrdom, carnivorous, voracious,
is pain twice over,
and the function of the purest grass, pain
twice over,
and the goodness of being pains us doubly.

Never, fellow humans,
has there been so much pain in the breast, in the lapel, in the
        wallet,
in the glass, in the butcher's, in arithmetic!
Never so much painful affection,
never has the distant rushed in so close,
never has fire ever
been better in its role as deathly cold!
Never, mr. minister of health, has health
been more deadly,
nor has migraine extracted so much forehead from the forehead!
And in the sideboard drawer, pain,
the heart, in its drawer, pain,
the lizard, in its drawer, pain.

Unhappiness is growing, brother humans,
more quickly than the machine, than ten machines, and it's
        growing
along with Rousseau's cattle, and our beards;

crece el mal por razones que ignoramos
y es una inundación con propios líquidos,
con propio barro y propia nube sólida!

Invierte el sufrimiento posiciones, da función
en que el humor acuoso es vertical
al pavimento,
el ojo es visto y esta oreja oída,
y esta oreja da nueve campanadas a la hora
del rayo, y nueve carcajadas
a la hora del trigo, y nueve sones hembras
a la hora del llanto, y nueve cánticos
a la hora del hambre y nueve truenos
y nueve látigos, menos un grito.

El dolor nos agarra, hermanos hombres,
por detrás, de perfil,
y nos aloca en los cinemas,
nos clava en los gramófonos,
nos desclava en los lechos, cae perpendicularmente
a nuestros boletos, a nuestras cartas;
y es muy grave sufrir, puede uno orar ...
Pues de resultas
del dolor, hay algunos
que nacen, otros crecen, otros mueren,
y otros que nacen y no mueren, otros
que sin haber nacido, mueren, y otros
que no nacen ni mueren (son los más).
Y también de resultas
del sufrimiento, estoy triste
hasta la cabeza, y más triste hasta el tobillo,
de ver al pan, crucificado, al nabo,
ensangrentado,

evil is growing for reasons we don't know
and it's a flood that brings its own liquids,
its own mud, and its own solid cloud!

Suffering inverts positions, making
the aqueous humor vertical
to the road,
the eye is seen and this ear heard,
and this ear chimes nine times at the hour
of lightning, and nine guffaws
at the hour of wheat, and nine female sounds
at the hour of weeping, and nine canticles
at the hour of hunger and nine thunderbolts
and nine lashes, minus a scream.

Pain grips us, brother humans,
from behind, from the side,
and drives us crazy in the movies,
nails us in gramophones,
unnails us in beds, falls perpendicularly
onto our tickets, onto our letters;
and it's a serious thing to suffer, one can pray . . .
But as a result
of pain, there are some
who are born, others grow, others die,
and others are born and don't die, others
who without being born die, and others
are neither born nor die (they're the majority).
And, as a result
of suffering, I am sad
to the top of my head, and even sadder down to my ankles,
to see the bread crucified, the turnip
bloodied,

llorando, a la cebolla,
al cereal, en general, harina,
a la sal, hecha polvo, al agua, huyendo,
al vino, un ecce-homo,
tan pálida a la nieve, al sol tan ardio!
¡Cómo, hermanos humanos,
no deciros que ya no puedo y
ya no puedo con tánto cajón,
tánto minuto, tánta
lagartija y tánta
inversión, tánto lejos y tánta sed de sed!
Señor Ministro de Salud: ¿qué hacer?
¡Ah! desgraciadamente, hombres humanos,
hay, hermanos, muchísimo que hacer.

the onion weeping,
the cereal, usually flour,
salt reduced to dust, water fleeing,
wine, an ecce homo,
so pale in the snow, so scorched in the sun!
How, brother humans,
can I not tell you that I can't bear it anymore and
that I can't bear so much drawer,
so much minute, so much
lizard, and so much
inversion, so much distance and so much thirst for thirst!
Mr. Minister of Health, what's to be done?
Ah, unfortunately, fellow humans,
brothers, there's a lot to do.

## Considerando en frío, imparcialmente...

Considerando en frío, imparcialmente,
que el hombre es triste, tose y, sin embargo,
se complace en su pecho colorado;
que lo único que hace es componerse
de días;
que es lóbrego mamífero y se peina...

Considerando
que el hombre procede suavemente del trabajo
y repercute jefe, suena subordinado;
que el diagrama del tiempo
es constante diorama en sus medallas
y, a medio abrir, sus ojos estudiaron,
desde lejanos tiempos,
su fórmula famélica de masa...

Comprendiendo sin esfuerzo
que el hombre se queda, a veces, pensando,
como queriendo llorar,
y, sujeto a tenderse como objeto,
se hace buen carpintero, suda, mata
y luego canta, almuerza, se abotona...

Considerando también
que el hombre es en verdad un animal
y, no obstante, al voltear, me da con su tristeza en la cabeza...

## "Considering coolly, impartially ..."

Considering coolly, impartially,
that man is sad, he coughs, and yet
takes pleasure in his inflamed chest;
that all he does is accumulate
days;
that he's a gloomy mammal and combs his hair ...

Considering
that man proceeds meekly from work,
reverberating boss, sounding subordinate;
that the diagram of time
is a constant diorama on his medals,
and that his half-closed eyes have studied,
since long long ago,
his famished formula for dough ...

Effortlessly understanding
that man does at times sit thinking,
as if about to weep,
and, subject to being laid out flat like an object,
he makes a good carpenter, sweats, kills,
and then sings, lunches, buttons himself up ...

Considering too
that man is, in truth, an animal,
and yet, when he turns round, he hits me on the head with
        his sadness ...

Examinando, en fin,
sus encontradas piezas, su retrete,
su desesperación, al terminar su día atroz, borrándolo ...

Comprendiendo
que él sabe que le quiero,
que le odio con afecto y me es, en suma, indiferente ...

Considerando sus documentos generales
y mirando con lentes aquel certificado
que prueba que nació muy pequeñito ...

le hago una seña,
viene,
y le doy un abrazo, emocionado.
¡Qué más da! Emocionado ... Emocionado ...

Finally, examining
his contradictory components, his lavatory,
his desperation, on finishing another awful day, erasing it ...

Understanding
that he knows I love him,
that I loathe him fondly and that to me he is, in short, a
          matter of complete indifference ...

Considering his general documents
and peering through one's glasses at that certificate
which proves that when he was born he was indeed tiny ...

I beckon him over,
he comes,
and I give him a hug, deeply moved.
Yes, what the heck! Moved ... deeply moved ...

## Sombrero, abrigo, guantes

Enfrente a la Comedia Francesa, está el Café
de la Regencia; en él hay una pieza
recóndita, con una butaca y una mesa.
Cuando entro, el polvo inmóvil se ha puesto ya de pie.

Entre mis labios hechos de jebe, la pavesa
de un cigarrillo humea, y en el humo se ve
dos humos intensivos, el tórax del Café,
y en el tórax, un óxido profundo de tristeza.

Importa que el otoño se injerte en los otoños,
importa que el otoño se integre de retoños,
la nube, de semestres; de pómulos, la arruga.

Importa oler a loco postulando
¡qué cálida es la nieve, qué fugaz la tortuga,
el cómo qué sencillo, qué fulminante el cuándo!

## Hat, Coat, Gloves

Opposite the Comédie Française is the Café
de la Régence; inside is a secluded
room, with an armchair and a table.
When I enter, the immovable dust has already got to its feet.

Between my lips made of rubber, the ember
of a cigarette smokes, and in the smoke you can see
two intensive smokes, the thorax of the Café,
and in the thorax, a thick rust of sadness.

It's important that autumn is grafted on to other autumns,
it's important that autumn blends in with the green shoots,
the cloud with semesters; the frown line with cheekbones.

It's important to smell like a madman postulating
how hot the snow is, how swift the tortoise,
how simple the how, how sudden the when!

## París, Octubre 1936

De todo esto yo soy el único que parte.
De este banco me voy, de mis calzones,
de mi gran situación, de mis acciones,
de mi número hendido parte a parte,
de todo esto yo soy el único que parte.

De los Campos Elíseos o al dar vuelta
la extraña callejuela de la Luna,
mi defunción se va, parte mi cuna,
y, rodeada de gente, sola, suelta,
mi semejanza humana dase vuelta
y despacha sus sombras una a una.

Y me alejo de todo, porque todo
se queda para hacer la coartada:
mi zapato, su ojal, también su lodo
y hasta el doblez del codo
de mi propia camisa abotonada.

*Paris, October 1936*


I am the only one leaving all this.
Leaving this bench, my pants,
my grand position, my actions,
my number split from end to end,
I am the only one leaving all this behind.

Whether from the Champs-Elysées or turning off down
that strange little Rue de la Lune,
there goes my demise, there goes my cradle,
and, surrounded by people, alone, free,
my human likeness turns around
and dispatches its shadows one by one.

And I'm leaving everything, because everything
remains to provide my alibi:
my shoe, its eyelet, as well as its mud,
and even the crease at the elbow
of my own buttoned-up shirt.

## Piedra negra sobre una piedra blanca

Me moriré en París con aguacero,
un día del cual tengo ya el recuerdo.
Me moriré en París—y no me corro—
tal vez un jueves, como es hoy, de otoño.

Jueves será, porque hoy, jueves, que proso
estos versos, los húmeros me he puesto
a la mala y, jamás como hoy, me he vuelto,
con todo mi camino, a verme solo.

César Vallejo ha muerto, le pegaban
todos sin que él les haga nada;
le daban duro con un palo y duro

también con una soga; son testigos
los días jueves y los huesos húmeros,
la soledad, la lluvia, los caminos …

## Black Stone on a White Stone

I'll die in Paris in a shower of rain,
a day I already hold in my memory.
I'll die in Paris—and I'm in no hurry—
perhaps on a Thursday, like today, in autumn.

Yes, it'll be a Thursday, because today, Thursday,
as I prose these verses, I had to struggle
to put on my humerus bones, and never before
have I turned, me and my road, to find myself alone.

César Vallejo is dead, they all beat him
even though he'd never done them any harm;
they hit him hard with a stick and hard, too,

with a rope; and the witnesses
are the Thursdays and my humerus bones,
the loneliness, the rain, the roads ...

*¡Y si después de tántas palabras...*


¡Y si después de tántas palabras,
no sobrevive la palabra!
¡Si después de las alas de los pájaros,
no sobrevive el pájaro parado!
¡Más valdría, en verdad,
que se lo coman todo y acabemos!

¡Haber nacido para vivir de nuestra muerte!
¡Levantarse del cielo hacia la tierra
por sus propios desastres
y espiar el momento de apagar con su sombra su tiniebla!
¡Más valdría, francamente,
que se lo coman todo y qué más da!...

¡Y si después de tánta historia, sucumbimos,
no ya de eternidad,
sino de esas cosas sencillas, como estar
en la casa o ponerse a cavilar!
¡Y si luego encontramos,
de buenas a primeras, que vívimos,
a juzgar por la altura de los astros,
por el peine y las manchas del pañuelo!
¡Más valdría, en verdad,
que se lo coman todo, desde luego!

Se dirá que tenemos
en uno de los ojos mucha pena
y también en el otro, mucha pena
y en los dos, cuando miran, mucha pena...
Entonces... ¡Claro!... Entonces... ¡ni palabra!

## "And if, after so many words..."

And if, after so many words,
the word doesn't survive!
If, after the birds' wings,
the motionless bird doesn't survive!
To be honest, it would be better
if it was all swallowed up, and there's an end to it!

Being born in order to live our death!
Waking up from the sky to the earth
by way of its own disasters
and watching for the moment to douse its shadow in its darkness!
Frankly, it would be better
if it was all swallowed up, and to hell with it!...

And, if after so much history, we succumb,
not to eternity,
but to those simple things, like being
at home or having a good think!
And if, afterwards, we discover,
out of the blue, that we live,
judging from the height of the stars,
by the comb and the stains on the handkerchief!
To be honest, it would be better
if it was, of course, all swallowed up!

Some will say that
in one eye there's a terrible sadness
and in the other eye too, a terrible sadness,
and in both, when they look, a terrible sadness ...
Then ... Of course!... Then ... Not a word!

*Va corriendo, andando, huyendo ...*


Va corriendo, andando, huyendo
de sus pies ...
Va con dos nubes en su nube,
sentado apócrifo, en la mano insertos
sus tristes paras, sus entonces fúnebres.

Corre de todo, andando
entre protestas incoloras; huye
subiendo, huye
bajando, huye
a paso de sotana, huye
alzando al mal en brazos,
huye
directamente a sollozar a solas.

Adonde vaya,
lejos de sus fragosos, cáusticos talones,
lejos del aire, lejos de su viaje,
a fin de huir, huir y huir y huir
de sus pies—hombre en dos pies, parado
de tánto huir—habrá sed de correr.

¡Y ni el árbol, si endosa hierro de oro!
¡Y ni el hierro, si cubre su hojarasca!
Nada, sino sus pies,
nada sino su breve calofrío,
sus paras vivos, sus entonces vivos ...

## *"Off he goes, running, walking, fleeing..."*

Off he goes, running, walking, fleeing
from his feet ...
Off he goes with two clouds on his one cloud,
apocryphally seated with, inserted in his hand,
his sad wherefores, his funereal therefores.

He's running from everything, walking
through colorless protests; he flees
upwards, he flees
downwards, he flees
at cassock-pace, he flees
lifting evil up in his arms,
he flees
directly so as to sob all alone.

Wherever he goes,
far from his rough, caustic heels,
far from the air, far from his journey,
in order to flee, flee and flee and flee
from his feet—a man on two feet, motionless
from so much fleeing—such a thirst for running.

And not the tree, if it passes itself off as gold!
Not iron, if it covers his tedious herbage!
Nothing, only his feet,
nothing, only a brief shiver,
his living wherefores, his living therefores ...

## Despedida recordando un adiós

Al cabo, al fin, por último,
torno, volví y acábome y os gimo, dándoos
la llave, mi sombrero, esta cartita para todos.
Al cabo de la llave está el metal en que aprendiéramos
a desdorar el oro, y está, al fin
de mi sombrero, este pobre cerebro mal peinado,
y, último vaso de humo, en su papel dramático,
yace este sueño práctico del alma.

¡Adiós hermanos san pedros,
heráclitos, erasmos, espinozas!
¡Adiós tristes obispos bolcheviques!
¡Adiós, gobernadores en desorden!
¡Adiós, vino que está en el agua como vino!
¡Adiós, alcohol que está en la lluvia!

¡Adiós también, me digo a mí mismo,
adiós, vuelo formal de los milígramos!
¡También adiós, de modo idéntico,
frío del frío y frío del calor!
Al cabo, al fin, por último, la lógica,
los linderos del fuego,
la despedida recordando aquel adiós.

## A Farewell Recalling a Goodbye

At the end, finally, ultimately,
I turn, I went back and, done for, I call out to you, giving you
my key, my hat, this little note addressed to you all.
At the end of the key is the metal with which we learned
to ungild gold, and there, at the end
of my hat, this poor disheveled brain,
and, ultimate glass of smoke, in its dramatic role,
lies this the soul's practical dream.

Goodbye, brother saint peters,
heraclituses, erasmuses, spinozas!
Goodbye, sad bolshevik bishops!
Goodbye, chaotic governors!
Goodbye, wine that is in the water like wine!
Goodbye, alcohol in the rain!

Goodbye too, I say to myself,
goodbye, formal flight of milligrams!
And goodbye too, in just the same way,
to the cold of the cold and the cold of the heat!
At the end, finally, ultimately, to logic,
to the frontiers of fire,
the farewell recalling that goodbye.

## Intensidad y altura

Quiero escribir, pero me sale espuma,
quiero decir muchísimo y me atollo;
no hay cifra hablada que no sea suma,
no hay pirámide escrita, sin cogollo.

Quiero escríbir, pero me siento puma;
quiero laurearme, pero me encebollo.
No hay toz hablada, que no llegue a bruma,
no hay dios ni hijo de dios, sin desarrollo.

Vámonos, pues, por eso, a comer yerba,
carne de llanto, fruta de gemido,
nuestra alma melancólica en conserva.

Vámonos! Vámonos! Estoy herido;
vámonos a beber lo ya bebido,
vámonos, cuervo, a fecundar tu cuerva.

27 OCTUBRE 1937

## Intensity and Height

I want to write but only foam comes out,
I want to say so many things, but I get stuck;
there's no spoken number that isn't a sum,
and no written pyramid without a heart.

I want to write, but feel like a puma,
I want to be crowned with laurels, but I'm stewing in onions.
There's no barking cough that doesn't end in mist,
and no god or son of god without development.

Let's go then and eat grass,
flesh of lamentation, fruit of sorrowing,
our melancholy soul preserved in a can.

Let's go! Let's go! I'm wounded;
let's go and drink what we've drunk already,
let's go, crow, and impregnate your mate.

27 OCTOBER 1937

## Un hombre pasa con un pan al hombro

Un hombre pasa con un pan al hombro
¿Voy a escribir, después, sobre mi doble?

Otro se sienta, ráscase, extrae un piojo de su axila, mátalo
¿Con qué valor hablar del psicoanálisis?

Otro ha entrado en mi pecho con un palo en la mano
¿Hablar luego de Sócrates al médico?

Un cojo pasa dando el brazo a un niño
¿Voy, después, a leer a André Bretón?

Otro tiembla de frío, tose, escupe sangre
¿Cabrá aludir jamás al Yo profundo?

Otro busca en el fango huesos, cáscaras
¿Cómo escribir, después del infinito?

Un albañil cae de un techo, muere y ya no almuerza
¿Innovar, luego, el tropo, la metáfora?

Un comerciante roba un gramo en el peso a un cliente
¿Hablar, después, de cuarta dimensión?

Un banquero falsea su balance
¿Con qué cara llorar en el teatro?

Un paria duerme con el pie a la espalda
¿Hablar, después, a nadie de Picasso?

## "A man walks past shouldering a stick of bread ..."

A man walks past shouldering a stick of bread
Am I going to write then about my double?

Another man sits down, scratches himself, extracts a louse
        from his armpit, kills it
What's the point of talking about psychoanalysis?

Another has entered my breast with a cudgel in his hand
Shall I speak to the doctor about Socrates?

A lame man walks by helped along by a child
Am I going to read André Breton after that?

Another is shivering with cold, coughing, spitting blood
Would it ever be right to refer to the inner I?

Another is searching in the mud for bones, peelings
How then write about the infinite?

A builder falls off a roof, dies, and won't eat lunch again
Why bother coming up with a new trope, a metaphor?

A storekeeper cheats a customer out of a gram
Can we really speak, then, about the fourth dimension?

A banker fiddles the books
How dare we weep at the theater?

An outcast falls asleep with one foot behind his back
Will anyone mention Picasso after that?

Alguien va en un entierro sollozando
¿Cómo luego ingresar a la Academia?

Alguien limpia un fusil en su cocina
¿Con qué valor hablar del más allá?

Alguien pasa contando con sus dedos
¿Cómo hablar del no-yó sin dar un grito?

5 NOVIEMBRE 1937

Someone goes to a funeral sobbing
How then enter the Academy?

Someone is cleaning a rifle in his kitchen
Do we dare speak of the afterlife?

Someone walks by counting on his fingers
How can we talk about the Not-I without screaming?

5 NOVEMBER 1937

## Me viene, hay días...

Me viene, hay días, una gana ubérrima, política,
de querer, de besar al cariño en sus dos rostros,
y me viene de lejos un querer
demostrativo, otro querer amar, de grado o fuerza,
al que me odia, al que rasga su papel, al muchachito,
a la que llora por el que lloraba,
al rey del vino, al esclavo del agua,
al que ocultóse en su ira,
al que suda, al que pasa, al que sacude su persona en mi alma.

Y quiero, por lo tanto, acomodarle
al que me habla, su trenza; sus cabellos, al soldado;
su luz, al grande; su grandeza, al chico.
Quiero planchar directamente
un pañuelo al que no puede llorar
y, cuando estoy triste o me duele la dicha,
remendar a los niños y a los genios.

Quiero ayudar al bueno a ser su poquillo de malo
y me urge estar sentado
a la diestra del zurdo, y responder al mudo,
tratando de serle útil en
lo que puedo, y también quiero muchísimo
lavarle al cojo el pie,
y ayudarle a dormir al tuerto próximo.

## "What comes to me on certain days..."

What comes to me on certain days is an abundant, political
      desire
to love, to kiss affection on both cheeks,
and what comes to me from afar is a demonstrative
love, another desire to love, whether they want me to or not,
the man who hates me, the one who tears up the little boy's
      piece of paper,
the woman who weeps for the man weeping,
the king of wine, the slave of water,
the one who hid behind his anger,
the one sweating, the one walking past, the one who shakes
      himself out in my soul.

And I therefore want to adjust the braid
of the one talking to me; the soldier's hair;
the great man's light; the small boy's greatness.
I immediately want to iron
a handkerchief for the man who cannot cry,
and, when I'm sad or when happiness pains me,
to patch up both children and geniuses.

I want to help the good man to be his little bit of badness
and I feel the urge to sit down
on the right side of the left-hander, and respond to the deaf-
      mute,
trying to be useful to him
as far as I can, and I also really really want
to wash the one-legged man's foot,
and lull to sleep my one-eyed neighbor.

¡Ah querer, éste, el mío, éste, el mundial,
interhumano y parroquial, proyecto!
Me viene a pelo,
desde el cimiento, desde la ingle pública,
y, viniendo de lejos, da ganas de besarle
la bufanda al cantor,
y al que sufre, besarle en su sartén,
al sordo, en su rumor craneano, impávido;
al que me da lo que olvidé en mi seno,
en su Dante, en su Chaplin, en sus hombros.

Quiero, para terminar,
cuando estoy al borde célebre de la violencia
o lleno de pecho el corazón, querría
ayudar a reír al que sonríe,
ponerle un pajarillo al malvado en plena nuca,
cuidar a los enfermos enfadándolos,
comprarle al vendedor,
ayudarle a matar al matador—cosa terrible—
y quisiera yo ser bueno conmigo
en todo.

6 NOVIEMBRE 1937

Ah, I want this, this to be mine, the universal,
interhuman, parochial project!
It suits me perfectly,
from the ground up, from the public groin up,
and, from far off, comes a desire to kiss
the singer's scarf,
to kiss on his frying pan the one who suffers,
as well as the deaf man undaunted inside his cranial murmurings,
and the one who gives me what I forgot was there in my breast,
on his Dante, on his Chaplin, on his shoulders.

I want, in conclusion,
when I'm poised on the celebrated brink of violence
or my heart is full of courage, I'd like
to help someone smiling to laugh out loud,
to place a little bird on the nape of the villain's neck,
to tend to the sick by annoying them,
to buy from the seller,
to help the killer to kill—how terrible—
and I'd like to be kind to myself
in every way.

6 NOVEMBER 1937

131

## El alma que sufrió de ser su cuerpo

Tú sufres de una glándula endocrínica, se ve,
o, quizá,
sufres de mí, de mi sagacidad escueta, tácita.
Tú padeces del diáfano antropoide, allá, cerca,
donde está la tiniebla tenebrosa.
Tú das vuelta al sol, agarrándote el alma,
extendiendo tus juanes corporales
y ajustándote el cuello; eso se ve.
Tú sabes lo que te duele,
lo que te salta al anca,
lo que baja por ti con soga al suelo.
Tú, pobre hombre, vives; no lo niegues,
si mueres; no lo niegues,
si mueres de tu edad ¡ay! y de tu época.
Y, aunque llores, bebes,
y, aunque sangres, alimentas a tu híbrido colmillo,
a tu vela tristona y a tus partes.
Tú sufres, tú padeces y tú vuelves a sufrir horriblemente,
desgraciado mono,
jovencito de Darwin,
alguacil que me atisbas, atrocísimo microbio.
Y tú lo sabes a tal punto,
que lo ignoras, soltándote a llorar.
Tú, luego, has nacido; eso
también se ve de lejos, infeliz y cállate,
y soportas la calle que te dio la suerte
y a tu ombligo interrogas: ¿dónde? ¿cómo?

## The Soul That Suffered from Being Its Body

You're suffering from your endocrine gland, that much is
            obvious,
or perhaps
you're suffering from me, from my sober, tacit sagacity.
You're afflicted by that diaphanous anthropoid just over there,
where the darkness is darkest.
You keep revolving around the sun, clasping your soul,
stretching out your bodily bunions
and adjusting your collar; that much is obvious.
You know what's hurting you,
what keeps leapfrogging over you,
what lowers itself through you on a rope to the ground.
You, poor man, are alive; don't deny it,
you're dying, don't deny it,
you're dying of your age, alas, and of your era.
And even though you weep, you drink,
and even though you bleed, you still feed your hybrid eyetooth,
your glum candle, and your private parts.
You're suffering, afflicted, and suffering horribly again,
unfortunate ape,
Darwin's youngest,
prying-eyed bailiff, vile microbe.
And you know it so well
that you ignore it, bursting into tears.
Therefore, you must have been born; that's
obvious too from a mile off, poor wretch, so shut up,
and make do with the street that chance gave you,
and ask your navel: where? how?

Amigo mío, estás completamente,
hasta el pelo, en el año treinta y ocho,
nicolás o santiago, tal o cual,
estés contigo o con tu aborto o conmigo
y cautivo en tu enorme libertad,
arrastrado por tu hércules autónomo ...
Pero si tú calculas en tus dedos hasta dos,
es peor; no lo niegues, hermanito.

¿Que nó? ¿Que sí, pero que nó?
¡Pobre mono!... ¡Dame la pata!... No. La mano, he dicho.

¡Salud! ¡Y sufre!

8 NOVIEMBRE 1937

My friend, you are completely,
to the roots of your hair, in the year nineteen thirty-eight,
nicolás or santiago, or whatever,
whether with yourself or your aborted self or with me
and captive in your vast liberty,
dragged along by your autonomous hercules.
But if you count on your fingers up to two,
it's even worse; don't deny it, little brother.

No? Yes, but no?
Poor ape!... Give me your paw!... No, your hand, I mean.

Cheers! And carry on suffering!

8 NOVEMBER 1937

## Palmas y guitarra

Ahora, entre nosotros, aquí,
ven conmigo, trae por la mano a tu cuerpo
y cenemos juntos y pasemos un instante la vida
a dos vidas y dando una parte a nuestra muerte.

Ahora, ven contigo, hazme el favor
de quejarte en mi nombre y a la luz de la noche tenebrosa
en que traes a tu alma de la mano
y huímos en puntillas de nosotros.

Ven a mí, sí, y a ti, sí,
con paso par, a vernos a los dos con paso impar,
marcar el paso de la despedida.
¡Hasta cuando volvamos! ¡Hasta la vuelta!
¡Hasta cuando leamos, ignorantes!
¡Hasta cuando volvamos, despidámonos!

¿Qué me importan los fusiles?
escúchame;
escúchame, ¿qué impórtanme,
si la bala circula ya en el rango de mi firma?
¿Qué te importan a ti las balas,
si el fusil está humeando ya en tu olor?
Hoy mismo pesaremos
en los brazos de un ciego nuestra estrella
y, una vez que me cantes, lloraremos.

## Palmas with Guitar

Now, with just the two of us, here,
come with me, lead your body by the hand,
and let's have supper together and, for a moment, live life
as two lives, giving a share of it to our death.

Now, come with yourself, and do me the favor
of complaining on my behalf, and by the light of the dark night
through which you're leading your soul by the hand,
we'll flee from ourselves on tiptoe.

Come to me, yes, and to you, yes,
in step, to see us both out of step,
keeping time until our farewell.
Until we return! Until next time!
Until we ignoramuses can read!
Until we come back, let's say farewell!

What do I care about guns?
listen to me;
listen to me, what do I care about them,
when the bullet is already within range of my signature?
What do you care about bullets,
if the gun can already sense your smell?
Today we'll weigh
our star in the arms of a blind man
and, as long as you sing to me, we'll cry.

———

*Palmas* here means specifically the rhythmic clapping that accompanies
singing or dancing.

Hoy mismo, hermosa, con tu paso par
y tu confianza a que llegó mi alarma,
saldremos de nosotros, dos a dos.
¡Hasta cuando seamos ciegos!
¡Hasta
que lloremos de tánto volver!
Ahora,
entre nosotros, trae
por la mano a tu dulce personaje
y cenemos juntos y pasemos un instante la vida
a dos vidas y dando una parte a nuestra muerte.

Ahora, ven contigo, hazme el favor
de cantar algo
y de tocar en tu alma, haciendo palmas.
¡Hasta cuando volvamos! ¡Hasta entonces!
¡Hasta cuando partamos, despidámonos!

8 NOVIEMBRE 1937

Today, my lovely, with your even step
and your confidence touched off by my alarm,
we'll step out from ourselves, two by two.
Until we're blind!
Until
we weep from so much returning!
Now,
between you and me, bring
your sweet being by the hand
and let's have supper together and, for a moment, live life
as two lives giving a share of it to our death.

Now, come with yourself, and be so kind
as to sing something
and to strum on your soul, keeping time by clapping.
Until we return! Until then!
Until we part, let's say farewell!

8 NOVEMBER 1937

## Sermón sobre la muerte

Y, en fin, pasando luego al dominio de la muerte,
que actúa en escuadrón, previo corchete,
párrafo y llave, mano grande y diéresis,
¿a qué el pupitre asirio? ¿a qué el cristiano púlpito,
el intenso jalón del mueble vándalo
o, todavía menos, este esdrújulo retiro?

¿Es para terminar,
mañana, en prototipo del alarde fálico,
en diabetis y en blanca vacinica,
en rostro geométrico, en difunto,
que se hacen menester sermón y almendras,
que sobran literalmente patatas
y este espectro fluvial en que arde el oro
y en que se quema el precio de la nieve?
¿Es para eso, que morimos tánto?
¿Para sólo morir,
tenemos que morir a cada instante?
¿Y el párrafo que escribo?
¿Y el corchete deísta que enarbolo?
¿Y el escuadrón en que falló mi casco?
¿Y la llave que va a todas las puertas?
¿Y la forense diéresis, la mano,
mi patata y mi carne y mi contradicción bajo la sábana?

## Sermon on Death

And, finally, moving straight to the domain of death,
which operates as a squadron, open parenthesis,
paragraph and key, a large hand, and dieresis,
why the Assyrian desk? why the Christian pulpit,
the intense pull of that vandalous piece of furniture
or, still less, this proparoxytone retreat?*

Is it so that it can all end
tomorrow, in a prototype of the phallic boast,
in diabetes and a white chamber pot,
in a geometrical face, in a corpse,
that a sermon and almonds are required,
that there are literally too many potatoes,
and this fluvial specter full of molten gold
and in which the price of the snow goes up in flames?
Is it for this that we die so much?
Is it simply for this
that we must die at every instant?
And the paragraph I'm writing?
And the deistic parenthesis I'm brandishing?
And the squadron where my helmet failed?
And the key that fits every door?
And the forensic dieresis, the hand,
my potato and my flesh and my contradiction under the sheets?

————

* *Proparoxytone* (in Spanish, *esdrújulo*): a term used to describe a word
in which the stress falls on the antepenultimate syllable, as in the
word itself. In Spanish, the stress normally falls on the penultimate
syllable.

¡Loco de mí, lovo de mí, cordero
de mí, sensato, caballísimo de mí!
¡Pupitre, sí, toda la vida; púlpito,
también, toda la muerte!
Sermón de la barbarie: estos papeles;
esdrújulo retiro: este pellejo.

De esta suerte, cogitabundo, aurífero, brazudo,
defenderé mi presa en dos momentos,
con la voz y también con la laringe,
y del olfato físico con que oro
y del instinto de inmovilidad con que ando,
me honraré mientras viva—hay que decirlo;
se enorgullecerán mis moscardones,
porque, al centro, estoy yo, y a la derecha,
también, y, a la izquierda, de igual modo.

8 DICIEMBRE 1937

Mad me, wolf me, lamb me,
most of all commonsensical horse me!
A desk, yes, all my life long; a pulpit too,
all my death long!
A barbarous sermon: these papers,
proparoxytonal retreat: this skin.

In this manner, cogitative, auriferous, biceps bulging,
I'll defend my prey twice over,
with my voice and also with my larynx,
and of the physical sense of smell with which I pray
and the instinct for immobility with which I walk
I'll feel proud for as long as I live—it must be said;
my blowflies will swell with pride,
because I stand at the very center, and to the right,
and, likewise, to the left.

8 DECEMBER 1937

## *de* España, aparta de mí este cáliz

*España, aparta de mí este caliz*

Niños del mundo,
si cae España—digo, es un decir—
si cae
del cielo abajo su antebrazo que asen,
en cabestro, dos láminas terrestres;
niños, ¡qué edad la de las sienes cóncavas!
¡qué temprano en el sol lo que os decía!
¡qué pronto en vuestro pecho el ruido anciano!
qué viejo vuestro 2 en el cuaderno!

¡Niños del mundo, está
la madre España con su vientre a cuestas;
está nuestra maestra con sus férulas,
está madre y maestra,
cruz y madera, porque os dio la altura
vértigo y división y suma, niños;
está con ella, padres procesales!

Si cae—digo, es un decir—si cae
España, de la tierra para abajo,
niños ¡cómo vais a cesar de crecer!
¡cómo va a castigar el año al mes!
¡cómo van a quedarse en diez los dientes,

## *from* Spain, Remove this Cup from Me

### Spain, remove this cup from me

Children of the world,
if Spain falls—I mean, let's just suppose—
if her forearm falls
from the sky and is caught,
in a sling, between two terrestrial plates;
children, what an age of concave temples!
how early beneath the sun is everything I told you!
how suddenly in your breast the ancient sound beats!
how very old your figure 2 looks there in your exercise book!

Children of the world, there
is mother Spain, her womb on her back;
there she is, our teacher, ruler at the ready,
there she is, mother and schoolmistress,
cross and wood, because she gave you height,
vertigo, and division and addition, children;
everything depends on her, O squabbling parents!

If she falls—I mean, let's just suppose—if Spain
falls down from the earth,
children, how you will cease to grow!
how the year will punish the month!
how your teeth will never be more than ten,

—

Published posthumously in 1939, these poems were written during
the first two years of the Spanish Civil War in praise of the ill-
equipped Republican militiamen fighting Franco's army.

en palote el diptongo, la medalla en llanto!
¡Cómo va el corderillo a continuar
atado por la pata al gran tintero!
¡Cómo vais a bajar las gradas del alfabeto
hasta la letra en que nació la pena!

Niños,
hijos de los guerreros, entre tanto,
bajad la voz, que España está ahora mismo repartiendo
la energía entre el reino animal,
las florecillas, los cometas y los hombres.
¡Bajad la voz, que está
con su rigor, que es grande, sin saber
qué hacer, y está en su mano
la calavera hablando y habla y habla,
la calavera, aquélla de la trenza,
la calavera, aquélla de la vida!

¡Bajad la voz, os digo;
bajad la voz, el canto de las sílabas, el llanto
de la materia y el rumor menor de las pirámides, y aún
el de las sienes que andan con dos piedras!
¡Bajad el aliento, y si
el antebrazo baja,
si las férulas suenan, si es la noche,
si el cielo cabe en dos limbos terrestres,
si hay ruido en el sonido de las puertas,
si tardo,
si no veis a nadie, si os asustan
los lápices sin punta, si la madre
España cae—digo, es un decir—
salid, niños del mundo; id a buscarla!…

the diphthong become a drumstick, the medal a lament!
How the lambkin will stay
tethered by one leg to the great inkwell!
How you will descend the steps of the alphabet
until you reach the letter where grief was born!

Children,
sons of fighters, meanwhile
lower your voices, because even now Spain is sharing out
her energy with the animal kingdom,
the little flowers, the comets, and the men.
Lower your voices, for she is
at her wits' end, not knowing
what to do, and in her hand she holds
the talking skull that talks and talks,
the skull, the one with the braid,
the skull, the skull of life!

Lower your voices, I tell you:
lower your voices, the song of the syllables, the lament
of matter and the softer murmur of the pyramids, as well as
the murmur of your temples weighed down by two stones!
Lower your breath, and if
her forearm falls,
if you hear the thwack of a ruler, if it's night,
if the sky fits into two terrestrial limbos,
if there's noise in the sound of the doors,
if I'm late,
if you don't see anyone, if you feel alarmed
by the blunt pencils, if mother
Spain falls—I mean, let's just suppose—
then go forth, children of the world; go and find her!

## IV

Los mendigos pelean por España,
mendigando en París, en Roma, en Praga
y refrendando así, con mano gótica, rogante,
los pies de los Apóstoles, en Londres, en New York, en Méjico.
Los pordioseros luchan suplicando infernalmente
a Dios por Santander,
la lid en que ya nadie es derrotado.
Al sufrimiento antiguo
danse, encarnízanse en llorar plomo social
al pie del individuo,
y atacan a gemidos, los mendigos,
matando con tan solo ser mendigos.

Ruegos de infantería,
en que el arma ruega del metal para arriba,
y ruega la ira, más acá de la pólvora iracunda.
Tácitos escuadrones que disparan,
con cadencia mortal, su mansedumbre,
desde un umbral, desde sí mismos, ¡ay! desde sí mismos.
Potenciales guerreros
sin calcetines al calzar el trueno,
satánicos, numéricos,
arrastrando sus títulos de fuerza,
migaja al cinto,
fusil doble calibre: sangre y sangre.
¡El poeta saluda al sufrimiento armado!

## IV

The beggars are fighting for Spain,
begging in Paris, in Rome, in Prague
and thus endorsing, in a pleading, gothic hand,
the feet of the Apostles, in London, in New York, in Mexico.
The mendicants are fighting, praying infernally
to God for Santander,
the joust in which no one is defeated.
They throw themselves
into the old suffering, furiously weeping leaden social tears
at the feet of the individual,
and they attack with their groans,
killing simply by being beggars.

Pleas from the infantry,
in which the weapon pleads from the metal up,
and sheer rage pleads too, on this side of the irascible gunpowder.
Tacit squadrons that fire forth,
in mortal cadence, their meekness,
from a doorway, from their own selves, yes, their very selves.
Potential warriors,
barefoot as they shoe themselves in thunder,
satanic, numeric,
dragging their titles behind them,
a crumb at their hip,
a double caliber gun: blood and blood.
The poet salutes their armed suffering!

## Pequeño responso a un héroe de la República

Un libro quedó al borde de su cintura muerta,
un libro retoñaba de su cadáver muerto.
Se llevaron al héroe,
y corpórea y aciaga entró su boca en nuestro aliento;
sudamos todos, el hombligo a cuestas;
caminantes las lunas nos seguían;
también sudaba de tristeza el muerto.

Y un libro, en la batalla de Toledo,
un libro, atrás un libro, arriba un libro, retoñaba del cadáver.

Poesía del pómulo morado, entre el decirlo
y el callarlo,
poesía en la carta moral que acompañara
a su corazón.
Quedóse el libro y nada más, que no hay
insectos en la tumba,
y quedó al borde de su manga el aire remojándose
y haciéndose gaseoso, infinito.

Todos sudamos, el hombligo a cuestas,
también sudaba de tristeza el muerto
y un libro, yo lo vi sentidamente,
un libro, atrás un libro, arriba un libro
retoño del cadáver ex abrupto.

10 SEPTIEMBRE 1937

*A brief prayer on the death of a hero of the Republic*

A book lay on the edge of his dead waist,
a book was sprouting forth from his dead corpse.
They carried the hero away,
and his corporeal, ill-fated mouth entered our breath;
we all sweated, our navels on our backs;
the wandering moons were following us;
the dead man, too, was sweating with sadness.

And in the battle of Toledo a book,
a book, a book behind, a book above, was sprouting from the
          corpse.

The poetry of the bruised cheekbone, half-spoken,
half-unsaid,
poetry in the moral letter accompanying
his heart.
Only the book remained and nothing else, for there are no
insects in the grave,
and on the edge of his sleeve the air was growing wet,
becoming vaporous, infinite.

We all sweated, our navels on our backs,
and the dead man, too, was sweating with sadness,
and a book, I saw it so feelingly,
a book, a book behind, a book above,
sprouted abruptly from the corpse.

10 SEPTEMBER 1937

151

## XII/*Masa*

Al fin de la batalla,
y muerto el combatiente, vino hacia él un hombre
y le dijo: "¡No mueras, te amo tanto!"
Pero el cadáver ¡ay! siguió muriendo.

Se le acercaron dos y repitiéronle:
"¡No nos dejes! ¡Valor! ¡Vuelve a la vida!"
Pero el cadáver ¡ay! siguió muriendo.

Acudieron a él veinte, cien, mil, quinientos mil,
clamando "¡Tanto amor y no poder nada contra la muerte!"
Pero el cadáver ¡ay! siguió muriendo.

Le rodearon millones de individuos,
con un ruego común: "¡Quédate hermano!"
Pero el cadáver ¡ay! siguió muriendo.

Entonces todos los hombres de la tierra
le rodearon; les vio el cadáver triste, emocionado;
incorporóse lentamente,
abrazó al primer hombre; echóse a andar ...

10 NOVIEMBRE 1937

## XII/Mass

At the end of the battle,
and the combatant dead, a man approached him
and said: "Don't die; I love you so much!"
But the corpse, alas, carried on dying.

Two other men went over to him and repeated that same plea:
"Don't leave us. Courage! Come back to life!"
But the corpse, alas, carried on dying.

Then twenty, a hundred, a thousand, five hundred thousand
men appeared, crying: "So much love, and yet it cannot
                overcome death!"
But the corpse, alas, carried on dying.

Millions of individuals gathered around him,
all with the same request: "Stay with us, brother, stay!"
But the corpse, alas, carried on dying.

Then all the men on the earth
gathered around him; the corpse saw them, sad and deeply
                moved,
and slowly got to his feet,
embraced the first man, and began to walk ...

10 NOVEMBER 1937

## XIV

¡Cuídate, España, de tu propia España!
¡Cuídate de la hoz sin el martillo,
cuídate del martillo sin la hoz!
¡Cuídate de la víctima a pesar suyo,
del verdugo a pesar suyo
y del indiferente a pesar suyo!
¡Cuídate del que, antes de que cante el gallo,
negárate tres veces,
y del que te negó, después, tres veces!
¡Cuídate de las calaveras sin las tibias,
y de las tibias sin las calaveras!
¡Cuídate de los nuevos poderosos!
¡Cuídate del que come tus cadáveres,
del que devora muertos a tus vivos!
¡Cuídate del leal ciento por ciento!
¡Cuídate del cielo más acá del aire
y cuídate del aire más allá del cielo!
¡Cuídate de los que te aman!
¡Cuídate de tus héroes!
¡Cuídate de tus muertos!
¡Cuídate de la República!
¡Cuídate del futuro!...

## XIV

Beware, Spain, of Spain itself!
Beware of the sickle without the hammer!
Beware of the hammer without the sickle!
Beware of the reluctant victim
of the reluctant executioner
and of the reluctant reluctant!
Beware of the one who, before the cock has crowed,
will deny you three times,
and of the one who, later on, denied you three times!
Beware of the skulls with no tibias,
and of the tibias with no skulls!
Beware of the new potentates!
Beware of the one eating your corpses,
of the one devouring your living dead!
Beware of the hundred percent loyal!
Beware of the sky this side of the air
and beware of the air on the other side of the sky!
Beware of those who love you!
Beware of your heroes!
Beware of your dead!
Beware of the Republic!
Beware of the future!...

# New Directions Paperbooks — a partial listing

**\*BILINGUAL EDITION**

For a complete listing, request a free catalog from New Directions, 80 8th Avenue, New York, NY 10011 or visit us online at ndbooks.com